Frank Richard Stockton

Captain Chap

Or, The rolling Stones

Frank Richard Stockton

Captain Chap
Or, The rolling Stones

ISBN/EAN: 9783337076658

Printed in Europe, USA, Canada, Australia, Japan

Cover: Foto ©ninafisch / pixelio.de

More available books at **www.hansebooks.com**

CAPTAIN CHAP

OR

The Rolling Stones

BY

FRANK R. STOCKTON

Author of "Rudder Grange," "A Jolly Fellowship," etc.

ILLUSTRATED BY
CHARLES H. STEPHENS

PHILADELPHIA
J. B. LIPPINCOTT COMPANY
1897

CONTENTS

CONTENTS

LIST OF ILLUSTRATIONS

1*

CAPTAIN CHAP

CHAPTER I.

"THE BEST THING YOU EVER HEARD OF."

IT was the month of October, and yet for the boys who belonged to the school of Mr. Wallace, in Boontown, the summer vacation was not yet over. Mr. Wallace had been taken sick, and although he was now recovering, it was not expected that he would be able to resume the labors of his school until about the middle of November.

Everybody liked Mr. Wallace, and very few of his patrons wished to enter their boys at another school when it was expected he would certainly re-open his establishment in the course of the fall. Most of his scholars, therefore, were pursuing their studies at home, according to methods which he recommended, and this plan was generally considered far more satisfactory than for the boys to go for a short time to other schools, where the systems of study were probably very different from those of Mr. Wallace.

It is true that some of the boys did not study very much during this extension of the vacation, but then it must be remembered that those who expect boys to do always everything that is right are very apt to be disappointed.

Philip Berkeley, who lived with his uncle, Mr. Godfrey Berkeley, at Hyson Hall, on the banks of one of Pennsylvania's most beautiful rivers, had studied a good deal since the time when his vacation should have ended, for he was a boy naturally inclined to that sort of thing, and he had, besides, the example of his uncle—who was hard at work studying law—continually before his eyes. But his two most particular friends, Chapman Webster and Phineas Poole, did not subject their school-books to any great amount of wear and tear.

Chap Webster was a lively, energetic boy, always ready to engage in some enterprise of work or play; and Phineas, generally called Phœnix by his companions, was such a useful fellow on his father's farm that he was usually kept pretty busy at one thing or another whenever he was at home.

At the time our story begins, Chap Webster had, for a week, been living in what he considered the most delightful kind of clover. He was a great lover of the water, although he had no particular desire for a mariner's life, in the ordinary sense of the term.

Accustomed since a child to the broad waters of the river, he had a great fancy for what might be called the inland marine service, and his highest ambition was to be captain of a tug-boat.

To course up and down the river in one of these swift and powerful little vessels, and to make fast to a great ship ever and ever so much larger than the "tug," and to tow her along against wind and tide, appeared to Chap a most delightful thing to do. There was a sense of power in it which pleased him.

He was now paying a visit to a relative in the city, who was one of the officers of a tug-boat company, and this gave Chap an opportunity to take frequent trips on his favorite vessels. He enjoyed all this so much that I fear he was in no hurry for his school to begin.

It was on a Monday afternoon that Philip and Phœnix were at the railroad station in Boontown. Each had come to town on an errand for his family, and they were now waiting for the three o'clock train from the city to come in.

The first person who jumped from the cars was

Chap Webster, and his feet had scarcely touched the platform before he spied his two friends.

"Hello, boys!" he cried, striding toward them. "I'm glad I found you here. I want to tell you the best thing you ever heard of! I'm going down to the Breakwater to-morrow on a tug-boat, and you two can go along if your folks will let you. I've fixed the whole thing up right. We'll be gone two days and a night. And I tell you what it is, boys, it will be more than glorious! We're going down after a big steamer, that's broken her propeller-blades and has to be towed up to the city. I came up to tell you fellows, and see what my people said about it. But I know they'll agree, and I don't want you to let your folks put in any objections. It'll be just as safe as staying at home, and there's entirely too much fun in it for any of us to miss it."

Neither Phil nor Phœnix hesitated for an instant in agreeing that Chap's idea was a splendid one.

Mr. Berkeley, Phil's uncle, when the subject was laid before him about an hour afterward, gave a hearty approval to the plan, for he was very glad that Phil should have an opportunity to enjoy an excursion of the kind.

His summer vacation had been filled up much more with work and responsibility than with recreation, and his uncle considered that a trip of some kind was certainly his due.

But the matter did not appear in the same light in the eyes of Mr. Poole. Now that Phœnix was not going to school, he thought it the boy's duty to make himself useful about the house and farm, and there were a great many things he wanted him to do.

When Phœnix came over to Hyson Hall early the next morning, and told Phil he didn't believe his father intended to let him go on this jolly old trip, Mr. Berkeley ordered his horse, Jouncer, to be saddled, and rode over to the Poole farm.

When he came back, he found Chap Webster with the other boys, and a noisy indignation meeting going on. He put a speedy stop to the proceedings, by informing the members of the small assemblage that Mr. Poole had consented to let Phœnix join the tug-boat party.

This news was received with a unanimous shout, and the boys separated to get ready as quickly as possible for the expedition, for they were to start for the city on the noon train.

"Take your heavy overcoats with you," said Mr. Berkeley, as Chap and Phœnix were bidding him a hasty good-by; "for it may be cold on the water at night, and you had better each take a change of linen with you, and some underclothes."

"What!" cried Phil; "for a little trip like this?"

"Yes," said Mr. Berkeley. "I am an old traveller, and I know that a great many things happen on these little trips. One of you may tumble overboard, and need a dry shirt, and at any rate you ought to feel that you may rough it as much as you please, and yet look clean and decent when you are coming home."

Hyson Hall was appointed for the rendezvous of the boys, and, after a slight luncheon, Joel drove them over to Boontown. But before they started Mr. Berkeley gave each of them a long, stout fishing-line, suitable for salt-water fishing.

"You may have a chance to use these," he said, "and I don't believe any of your own lines are strong enough for deep-water work."

He gave Phil a pocket lantern and a tin box of matches, with a paper of extra fish-hooks and various other little articles, which might be of use.

"If I'd been going by myself," said Chap, "I'd have just clapped on my hat, and started for town."

"Yes," said Phœnix, "and then, when you got a chance to fish, you'd have growled because you hadn't a line. I tell you what it is, Phil, your uncle knows what he is about. I wish I knew what he said to father."

"Some magic words," said Chap; "but you needn't think anybody is ever going to tell them to you. You'd go round slinging spells over your whole family, and having everything your own way. I rather think you'd have an easy time of it."

"Yes," said Phœnix, "you're about right, and when any work turned up that I wanted to do, I'd chuck a spell over a long-legged fellow named Chap Webster, and make him come and help."

"Joel," said Chap, "hadn't you better touch up the noble beast? We don't want to be late, you know."

"We'll get there soon enough," said Joel. "I drive on time, and I never miss trains."

"If you hurry up people that way, Chap," said Phil, "you'll have this trip over sooner than you want it to be."

"You needn't worry your mind about that," said Chap. "When we get on the real trip, I'm the fellow to help stretch it out as far as it will go."

The trip down the river and bay was quite as enjoyable as the boys had expected it to be. The little tug was not very commodious, and not very clean, but there was a small after-deck, on which they could lounge quite comfortably.

The boys had never been far below the city, and the scenery was novel and interesting to them. Chap would have been glad to have the tug stop occasionally, so that they could have a chance to fish; but he had sense enough not to propose anything of the kind to the captain.

They reached their destination the next day, and it was then found that the steamer with the broken propeller was not quite ready to be towed up; and it was decided not to start with her on her trip up the river until the following morning.

In the course of the afternoon, however, some work appeared for the captain of the tug-boat. Far out to sea a schooner was perceived, with her foremast and part of her bowsprit gone, and endeavoring, against a head-wind, to make her way to the refuge of the Breakwater.

There was a strong wind blowing from the north, with a chance of its getting farther to the east before long, and it was considered doubtful whether the disabled schooner would be able to get in before a storm came on.

"Boys," said the captain, coming aft to where our friends were sitting, "I've made up my mind to go out and offer to tow that schooner in. I might as well be making some money for the company as to lie here doing nothing. But I think it's going to be pretty rough, and, if you fellows don't care to go along, I'll put you ashore."

The boys, who had been so much interested in everything around them that they had not even taken out their fishing-lines, cried out at once that they would not think of going ashore. Nothing would please them more than a trip out to sea.

"The rougher the better!" cried Chap. "I just want to feel what it is like to be tossed on the ocean wave."

"All right!" said the captain, with a grin. "We'll toss you."

CHAPTER II.

A SEA VOYAGE.

It was not long after this little conversation that the tug-boat was bravely puffing out to sea. The wind was strong and the waves ran pretty high, but the boat made her way over the rough water without difficulty.

The boys were delighted with the motion of the vessel as it plunged over the waves, and none of them felt in the least degree sick.

Chap wished to go out on the bow, where he could stand and see the boat " breast the billows;" but he was not allowed to do this, for every now and then a shower of spray came over the bows, and he would have been drenched to the skin in ten minutes. Even where they sat in the stern, the boys were frequently treated to a shower of spray; but this, as they wore their overcoats, they did not mind in the least.

It took them longer to near the schooner than they had supposed it would, for she was making very slow headway against the wind, and in some of her long tacks she seemed to the boys as if she were trying to keep out of their way.

At last, however, they reached her, and the tug steamed close enough to her side to allow the people on board to be hailed. But, to the disgust of the captain of the tug-boat, his offers to tow the disabled vessel into shelter were declined.

Her captain believed that he could work her in without any help, and he did not wish to incur the expense of being towed.

"All right, then!" said the captain of the tug-boat to the boys, who stood near him. "She can run in by herself, and perhaps she'll make the Breakwater in a week or two. We have lost nothing but some of our owners' coal, and you fellows have had a sea trip. And now we will run back again."

The captain made two mistakes that day. One was when he thought he was going to make some money by towing a schooner and the other was when he thought he was going to run in again.

The tug-boat had not gone ten minutes on her returning course, when suddenly her machinery stopped, and in a few moments the boat turned about and began to roll in the trough of the sea.

There was now a good deal of confusion in the

engine-room, and there the boys made their way, not without difficulty, for the rolling motion of the boat made it very hard for them to keep their feet.

In the engine-room they found the captain, the engineer, and one or two others of the small crew. Something had broken, the boys knew not what, for no one seemed to have time to explain the matter to them.

Efforts were being made to repair the injury. There was a great deal of hammering and banging and loud talking, and presently the engine let off the steam from the boiler, which made such a noise it was almost impossible to hear anything that was not shouted into one's ear.

Perceiving that they were in the way, and could find out nothing, and were to be told nothing, the boys prudently retired into the inner cabin. Here Phil and Chap became quite sick. They could stand the pitching and tossing of the boat as she rose over and plunged down the waves, but this rolling motion was too much for them.

The two unfortunates crawled into the little bunks in which they had slept the night before, while Phœnix, with an air of brave resignation, braced himself against the cabin-door, and waited to see what would happen next.

Nothing seemed to happen next. After awhile the noise of the escaping steam grew less, and then it stopped. The hammering and banging had also ceased, and thinking that everything was all right now, Phœnix went forward to see how things were going on.

It was not easy to see much, for the engine-room was lighted only by a hanging lantern, but he met the captain, who informed him that they were in a bad way. One of the connecting-rods had been broken, and as the engine was not stopped soon enough, some other parts of the machinery had been damaged.

"We have tried to patch her up," said the captain, "but it is no go. All we can do is to make everything tight, and lie here until some vessel comes along to give us a tow in. This has been a pretty bad day for us, for we're not going to take any steamer up the river to-morrow."

"How long do you think you'll have to stay here?" asked Phœnix.

"Don't know," answered the captain. "Something may come along pretty soon, and we may not be towed in till morning. But you needn't be afraid. We'll make everything tight, and though we may roll and pitch, we won't take in any water."

"I suppose that vessel with a broken mast couldn't help us?" said Phœnix.

"No," said the captain, "it is more than she can do to take care of herself, and she is out of sight now, although she isn't any nearer the Breakwater than we are."

"Perhaps some steamboat will come out after us when they find we don't come back," suggested Phœnix.

"That may be," said the captain, willing to give his young passengers as much encouragement as possible. "But you fellows had better get something to eat, and turn in. You'll be more comfortable in your bunks while we are rolling about in this way."

But Chap and Phil did not want anything to eat. The very idea was horrible to them. And so Phœnix ate his hard biscuit and some cold meat, for there seemed to be no intention of even boiling a pot of coffee, and then he crawled into his little bunk.

"Boys," groaned Chap, "I don't care for a tugboat as much as I used to."

"Care for it!" said Phil, in a weak voice. "I hope I may never——"

And here his remark ended; he was too sick to say what he hoped.

The night was a horrible one. Occasionally the boys slept; but as they found, whenever they dropped into a doze, they were very apt to roll out of their bunks, they were obliged to keep awake most of the time. As soon as daylight appeared, they were all anxious to go outside, feeling

The rescue.

that a breath of fresh air would be better than anything else in the world. This the captain, who seemed to have been up all night, would not allow.

"You'd be washed overboard," he said, "and things are bad enough as they are, without any of you getting drowned. There's a regular gale off shore, and we haven't sighted an inward-bound steamer yet."

In the course of an hour or two, it was evident that a vessel ought to be sighted very soon, for the tug, which was not built for such rough work as this, had, in spite of the efforts of the crew to make everything tight on the decks, shipped a good deal of water, and it was necessary to work the pumps. But this did not help matters, for it was found that a leak had sprung somewhere, and the water came in faster than it could be pumped out.

The tug was now far from the land, and in the path of coastwise steamers; and before noon the welcome sight of a line of smoke appeared on the horizon. It was a steamer which was approaching them, but, unfortunately, it was going southward, and not northward.

"She's a Savannah steamer," said the captain, "but we've got to git on board of her, no matter where she is going; for this old boat can't stand this sort of thing much longer. We've been blowing out from shore all night, and there's no time for anything to come out after us now."

The boys looked aghast.

"Savannah!" they cried. "We don't want to go to Savannah!"

"It's a good sight better place than the bottom of the ocean," said the captain.

It was a bad bargain for the boys, but they had to make the best of it.

"What are you going to do in Savannah?" asked Phœnix, in a tone of dismay.

"It can't take us more than a couple of days to get there," said Phil, "and then we can telegraph home. As soon as our folks know where we are, I shall feel that everything is all right."

"I shan't feel that anything is all right until we know where we are ourselves," said Chap, looking out of one of the little windows of the cabin. "Did you ever see such a pokey old steamer as that is? I believe we shall sink before she gets to us."

But this unfortunate event did not happen, although the tug was very deep in the water and rolling heavily when the steamer lay to, with her bow to the wind, a few hundred yards away from them.

A large boat was speedily lowered and rowed to the tug. In less than half an hour the unfortunate occupants of the sinking tug-boat had been taken on the steamer.

A few articles were brought away from the tug, and the boys were allowed to carry with them their valises.

As soon as the boat-load of people was on the steamer, and the boat hauled up to its davits, the vessel put about, and proceeded on her way.

As the boys looked back, they saw the little tug, with her smoke-stack very much on one side, and but little of her hull visible, tossing and pitching on the waves.

"She isn't good for another half-hour," said the engineer, who stood by.

The party rescued from the sinking tug-boat was very kindly received on board the steamer, but it was quite evident, even to the hopeful and enthusiastic Chap, that there was no intention of putting back for the Breakwater.

The boys had never been on an ocean steamer before, and would have been greatly delighted with their present experience had it not been for the feeling that every movement of the ponderous engine beneath them was taking them farther and farther from their homes.

It would be impossible for their friends to hear from them for at least two days, and the news that the tug-boat had gone out to sea, and never returned, would probably reach Boontown very soon.

All three were very much dejected when they

thought of the misery and grief which the intelligence would cause in their families, and Phœnix
seemed more downcast than either of the others.

"If father believes I'm drowned," he said, "it'll
be just his way to go about grieving that he worked
me too hard. I know I made him think that, but
I didn't do so much after all."

"If my folks look at the thing in that light,"
said Chap, "they'll grieve that they didn't get
more out of me before I was drowned."

"I don't believe there'll be as much mourning
as you think," said Phil. "Uncle will be on
hand, and he's been in so many scrapes, and pulled
through them all, that he knows just about how
things will turn up. I bet it won't be half an
hour after he hears the news before he thinks out
the whole thing, and has made all your people see
that it's as clear as daylight that we've been carried out to sea, and picked up by some steamer,
and that we'll be heard from soon after she gets
to her port. He'll know that there wasn't storm
enough to wreck a good, stout tug-boat, and that
something must have got out of order, so that she
was carried out to sea."

"If that one-masted schooner ever got in," said
Phœnix, "she'd let them know there was something
wrong with us, for she must have seen or heard us
blowing off steam."

"I don't know about that," said Chap, "for

before I turned into my sick-bed, the vessel was pretty well out of sight. We were going in opposite directions, as well as I could make out."

"That was because she was sailing against the wind, and had to make long tacks," said Phœnix.

"Do you suppose I didn't know that?" asked Chap, drawing himself up in such an erect position that a great lurch of the vessel nearly threw him off his feet.

"We might as well make the best of it," said Phil, "and have a good time. In a couple of days we will be in Savannah, and when we have telegraphed home, everybody'll be all serene, if they are not now."

"Your head's level, Phil," said Chap. "Let's go and explore the ship."

On the breezy deck of the steamer, none of the boys felt in the least degree sea-sick, and they went about in high spirits. The purser, a good-natured man, took them in charge, and showed them the engine-room and various parts of the vessel, but it was not long before he gave them a piece of information which nearly took their breath away.

In answer to an inquiry in regard to the time at which they might expect to reach Savannah, the purser told them that the vessel could not stop at that port at all. The captain of the tug-boat had been right in saying that this was a Savannah steamer, but she had been temporarily withdrawn from that line, and was now bound for Nassau, in the Bahamas.

"When will we get there?" asked Chap. "Can we telegraph from Nassau?"

"We shall reach Nassau in about four days," said the purser, "but there is no cable from those islands. You will have to carry the news of your safety yourselves when we bring you back to New York."

"Can't we send a letter?" asked Phil.

"Not any sooner than you can come yourselves," said the purser, "for we shall bring back the mail from Nassau to the United States."

"And how long will it be before you get back to New York?" asked Phil.

"I don't know just how long we shall lie at Nassau," said the good-natured purser; "but I think it will be ten or twelve days before we are in New York again."

"Won't we meet some ship that will take us back or carry a letter?" asked Phœnix.

"I can't say," replied the purser. "The captain will do what he can for you, but I don't know that he will have a chance of putting you on board a northern-bound steamer, or of sending news of you to your friends."

CHAPTER III.

"A CONTINENT BEFORE US."

IT was very hard for the boys to get their spirits up after the news they had just heard.

"Ten days before our folks hear from us!" ejaculated Phœnix. "That's simply dreadful! They'll give us up long before that time."

"We will find them all in black when we get back," said Chap, with a doleful face.

But even this gloomy prospect could not long depress the spirits of our young friends.

By the next morning they were going about cheerfully, hoping and believing that something would soon turn up by which they could speedily get back to their friends, or, at least, send news of their safety.

The weather was now fine, although it was so cool that they were obliged to wear their overcoats whenever they were on deck, and they could not help enjoying this unexpected sea voyage.

They did not see much of the tug-boat people. These men lived forward with the crew of the steamer, while the boys ate and slept with the passengers.

On the morning of the third day of their steamer trip, they met one of the tug-boat crew,—a man named Adam Guy. This man had been the only person on board the tug-boat to whom the boys had taken any particular fancy. He had been a sailor, had visited many parts of the world, and had a great deal to tell of his various experiences on the sea and land. He was a strong and wiry, but not very large, man; and, like many sailors, he wore little gold rings in his ears. His hair was thin and sandy, and hung in short curls at the back of his head. He had a pleasant smile, and appeared to be an easy-going, good-tempered fellow.

"Young men," said Adam, "I've been a-wantin' to see you and have a little talk with you. Do you know there's no chance of our meetin' any vessels, or of your bein' sent home or gettin' any word back, either?"

"How is that?" asked the boy.

"Why, it's just this. We're out of the way now of all craft bound north. I did think we might a' met a coast steamer yesterday or the day before; but if we did, we passed them in the night, for I didn't see any. We are now off the coast of

Florida, and as we are sailin' south, we keep pretty well in shore, so as to be out of the way of the Gulf Stream, which runs northward, you know; and, as you've lived on a big river, you understand what it is to sail agin a strong tide. But, of course, every vessel bound north tries to keep in the current of the Gulf Stream, so's to be helped along. So, just about here, where the Gulf Stream is near our coast, you find all vessels, goin' south, keepin' pretty near shore, and them bound north, far out. It won't be long before we're near enough to the coast for you to see the trees. And we'll run down till we git about opposite Jupiter light, and then we'll sail across the stream and make straight for the Bahamas. I know all about these waters, for I've sailed in them often. Now, as for me, I don't want to go to Nassau, and I don't believe you want to, either. The captain of our tug and the rest of our men are all willin' to go, and ship on this steamer for their home trip. They'll be short o' hands then, for some of the crew are to be discharged at Nassau, but I don't want to go to that old English town. I've been there, and I've had enough of it."

"But what are we going to do?" asked Phil. "We can't jump overboard and swim ashore."

"No," said Adam, "we can't do that, but I've a plan in my head. Before we git to Jupiter light, the water is so deep near the coast that steamers often run in very close. Now, if the captain would lie-to there and send you fellers and me ashore in a boat, it would be the best thing he could do for us."

" What would we do when we got there ?" asked the boys.

" Do ?" said Adam. " Why we'd all go North, and lose no time about it, instead of goin' over to the Bahamas and stayin' there, I don't know how long, and then takin' a week for the home trip. Just back of the coast-line, down there, is the Indian River, and sometimes it's not much more'n a stone's throw from the beach. If we could be landed, we could easily git over to that, and there we'd find a craft to take us up to Titusville, and from that place we'd easy git over to the St. John's River, and then you boys could telegraph home. I've travelled all through that part of Florida, and I could take you along as straight as a bee-line. There are settlements here and there on the Indian River, and you needn't be afraid but we'll be taken good care of till we git to Titusville. After that it'll be all plain sailin'."

" I'd like that plan first-rate," said Chap.

" And so would I !" cried both of the other boys.

" But do you think the captain would stop," asked Phil, " and put us off ?"

" That's what's got to be found out," said Adam.

" If I was you fellers I'd just go to him and ask about it. Lay the p'ints before him strong, and let him know how much you want to send word to your friends where you are, and then to git along home as quick as possible. Tell him I'll go along with you and pilot you through all straight."

The boys agreed that this plan was a capital one, and, after a little consultation, they decided to go and talk to the captain about it, and make Phil the spokesman.

At first, the captain did not take very kindly to the proposition. He did not wish to lose time, nor to incur the trouble and risk of sending a boat on shore. He also knew that a great part of the coast of Florida was nothing but a barren waste, and he did not think it would be any great kindness to the persons he had saved from drowning to put them on shore to suffer from exposure and privation. But, on the other hand, if the boys were landed in Florida, they would be at least in their own country, and ought to be able to communicate with their friends much sooner than if he took them along with him to the foreign islands to which he was bound.

" You would need money," he said, "after you get ashore, for you couldn't expect the people there to take care of you, and carry you about free of charge; and, although I am willing to give you a berth here, I can't supply you with cash for a land trip."

"I have some money," said Phil, "though not very much."

"And I've got——" said Chap, thrusting his hands into his pocket.

"Oh, there's plenty of money," interrupted Phœnix. "There need be no trouble about that."

"Well, then," said the captain, who was beginning to see some sense in the proposition of the boys, "one difficulty is removed. Suppose you go forward and send that man you spoke of to me."

The captain had a long conversation with Adam, and convinced himself that that individual knew what he was talking about when he proposed his plan. The captain of the tug-boat was called in, and Adam's trustworthiness seemed well established.

After consultation with some of the other officers, it was decided to put the boys and Adam Guy ashore when a suitable place should be reached. The news created considerable excitement among the passengers, and great interest was taken in the proposed landing of the boys.

The air in these semi-tropical waters was warm and balmy, and the sea was smooth. Everything seemed favorable for going on shore. About four o'clock in the afternoon the ship lay to about half a mile from a broad, sandy beach. This locality Adam declared he knew very well.

The Indian River, he said, lay but a short distance back, behind a narrow forest of palmettos; and at the distance of a mile or two there was a house on the river bank, where shelter could be obtained until they could get transportation up the river.

The captain, however, took care that the little party should not suffer in case they did not reach shelter as soon as they expected. He provided them with provisions suitable for two days, put up in four convenient packages. Each carried a canteen of fresh water, and Adam took charge of a large tarpaulin, rolled up into a compact bundle, which could be used as a protection in case of rain. The weather was so mild that their overcoats would be sufficient to keep them warm at night.

While the men were preparing to lower a boat, Phil took Phœnix aside, and asked him what he meant by saying there was plenty of money.

"Chap has only three dollars," he said, "and I haven't that much."

"I have fifty dollars," said Phœnix, "and I guess that will take us along till we can telegraph for more."

"How did you come to have that much?" asked Phil, with surprise.

c

"Why, you see, our folks haven't settled what is to be done with some money I got for helping to run the "Thomas Wistar" ashore, and father is taking care of it. But I made up my mind that I was going to keep hold of some of it myself. A fellow likes to feel that he has got something of his own that he can lay hands on, no matter what is done with the general pile. So I locked up fifty dollars in my room, and when we started off, I didn't want to leave it behind, for I didn't know but the house might burn down. So I put it in an old money-belt father used to wear, and it's strapped around me now."

"You're a gay old fellow!" said Chap, who had come up and heard this. "You are always turning up at the right time."

"And right side up," said Phil.

A few minutes after this, a large boat, pulled by four men, and containing Adam Guy and our three friends, was leaving the side of the steamer, followed by the cheers of the passengers, who had assembled on the decks to bid the little party farewell.

The sea was quiet, with the exception of a long and gentle swell, and the first part of the little trip seemed like rowing on a river. But when they neared the shore and saw the long lines of surf rolling in front of them, the boys began to feel a little uneasy. This was something entirely novel to them, and, although they were not exactly afraid, they could not say that they felt altogether comfortable at the idea of going through these roaring breakers.

But the surf at this point was not really very high, and the boat was a metallic one, with air compartments at each end, and the men rowed steadily on, appearing to have no more fears of the breakers than of the open sea.

As the boat reached the first line of surf and was lifted up and carried swiftly forward on its great back, and then dropped into a watery hollow, to be raised again by another wave and carried still farther on, our boys held tightly to the sides of the boat as if they felt they must stick to that craft, whatever happened. But the men pulled steadily on, keeping the boat's head straight for the shore.

The breakers came rolling on behind as if they would sweep over the boat and cover her up with their dark green water, but another wave seemed always underneath to carry her on beyond the reach of the one which followed, and it was not long before, by the aid of oars and the incoming surf, they gained the beach.

Before the wave which had carried them in began to recede, Adam and another man jumped into the water and pulled the boat well up on the sands.

Then the whole party disembarked, Chap jumping into water ankle-deep, and giving a shout that might have been heard on the steamer.

As soon as the boys' valises and the other traps had been put ashore, the boat was turned about, and, with Adam's help, was launched into the surf.

The pull back through the breakers was harder than the coming in, but the four men knew their business, and the stanch life-boat easily breasted every line of surf.

In five minutes they were out in smooth water and pulling hard for the steamer. As soon as they reached it the boat was hauled up, the vessel was put about, and with a farewell blast from her steam-whistle, she proceeded on her way.

"Hurrah!" cried Chap, waving his cap over his head. "Now I feel that we are really our own masters, and that we're going to have the rarest old time we've ever known. Boys, the whole continent is before us!"

"That's the trouble of it," said Phil. "If there wasn't quite so much continent before us we might expect to get home sooner."

"Trouble? Home?" cried Chap. "Don't let anybody mention such things to me. I'm gayer than the larkiest lark that ever flapped himself aloft!"

And, with these words, he ran to the top of a

little sand hillock to see as much of the continent as he could.

"If I were you fellers," said Adam, "I'd make that young man captain. You'll never be able to manage him if you don't let him go ahead."

"Good!" said Phil; "let's make him captain, and you, Phœnix, ought to be treasurer, for you carry the funds."

"And what'll you be?" asked Phœnix.

"You're mixin' up your officers," said Adam; "but as a party of this kind is a little out of the general run, I guess it won't matter. As this is a land expedition," he said to Phil, "you might be quartermaster, and I'll be private."

"All right!" cried the boys.

And when Chap came running down from the sand-hill he was informed of the high position to which he had been chosen.

"My friends," cried Chap, drawing himself up and clapping his breast with his hand, "you do me honor, and I'll lead you—I'll lead you——"

"Into no end of scrapes," suggested Phil.

"Perhaps you're right. That may be so. But you're bound to follow," said Captain Chap.

"He'll lead you sure enough," laughed Adam. And then he added to himself, forgetting that this was a land, and not a nautical expedition, "I'll keep my hand upon the tiller."

CHAPTER IV.

WITH HOOK AND LINE.

AFTER standing for a few moments to take a last look at the steamer, which was now rapidly making her way southward, our party prepared to take up the shortest line of march for the Indian River.

The boys slung their overcoats and valises over their shoulders, and these, with their water-canteens and provisions, made for each of them a pretty good load. But Adam had a still heavier burden, for he carried the roll of tarpaulin in addition to his other traps.

"I am not captain," said Adam, addressing Chap, "but I'll go ahead, for I'll be able to find my way over to the river better than you will."

"All right," said Chap. "Adam was the first man, and you can take the lead. But I am captain, for all that, and I expect to be obeyed."

"Expect away," said Phil; "it'll keep your mind busy, and stop you from making plans for blowing us all up North in one bang."

"Silence!" cried Chap. "Forward, march!"

The way from the beach back to the river was a very hard one, and a good deal longer than Adam had expected it to be.

For a time they walked over loose, soft sand, which was piled into little hills by the wind, then they came to a thick growth of palmetto-trees, the ground being covered with underbrush of the most disagreeable kind, consisting mainly of a low bush, called the "saw-palmetto," which was made up of leaves three or four feet long, with sharp teeth at each edge.

A variety of tangled vines, concealing rotten palmetto stumps, of all sizes, helped to make the walking exceedingly difficult. But some man or animal had been that way before, and through the almost undistinguishable path, which Adam seemed to scent out, rather than to see, the party slowly made its way.

When at last they reached the river, the boys gave a great shout, but Adam merely grinned, and looked anxiously up and down.

The broad, smooth waters of the Indian River spread before the delighted eyes of our young friends. Large birds were flying through the air. At a little distance hundreds of ducks were swimming on the water. The low shores were green and beautiful. But what Adam looked for was not there.

As far as the eye could reach—and as the river here bent away from them on either hand, they could see the bank on which they stood for a long distance up and down—not a house, or clearing, or sign of human habitation, could be seen, and on the river there was not a sail or boat.

"I haven't struck just the place I want to get to," said Adam, "for the house I'm after is just above this bend where the river turns due north agen; but then it couldn't be expected I'd pick out the very place I wanted when I was on board a steamer nearly a mile from shore. If I could 'a' seen the river, I'd been all right, but beaches is pretty much alike."

"I think you did very well," said Phil, "to get so near the place. The end of that bend can't be so very far away."

"It wouldn't be much of a walk," said Adam, "if there was a good beach at the side of the river. There's a sandy shore on the other side, as you can see, but that's no good to us. Along here, for pretty much the whole bend, you see the trees and underbrush grow right down to the water, and it would be wadin' and sloppin', as well as scratchin'."

"We might keep farther in shore," said Chap, "where we could find dry walking."

"It would be dry enough, but it would be mighty slow," said Adam. "The best and quickest thing we can do is to get right back to the beach. There we'll find good, hard walkin', and we can tramp along lively till we calkilate we're about opposite John Brewer's place, and then we can push through agen to the river."

"I guess that's about the best thing to do," said Phil, "for it will give us less of this horrid jungle-scratching than trying to push right straight along through the woods."

"All right!" cried Chap. "Backward! March!"

And again, with Adam at the head, the party pushed through the strip of woods which separated the river from the ocean-beach. The march along the sand was easy enough, but it seemed very long.

"Why, I thought," cried Chap, "that it was only a little way to the end of that bend!"

"It's further than it looks," said Adam. "I've got a pretty good notion how fur we ought to walk before we strike across; but it won't be long before we try the woods agen."

In about ten minutes, Adam turned, and led the way toward the river. The strip of land was much narrower here than where they had crossed it before, and after a short season of scrambling and

4*

scratching and pushing over ground where it seemed as if no one had ever passed before, the river was reached. Here was a broad strip of clean sand lying between the woods and the water's edge, but there was no house in sight.

"Isn't this the end of the bend?" asked Phœnix.

"Yes, it's the end of the bend," said Adam, looking about him; "but it's the wrong bend. I know the place now just as well as if I'd been born here. You see the river makes another bend up there, don't you? It's a good while since I've been here, and I never came to the place by the way of the sea. The house we're after is up there. There's no mistake this time."

"But that must be ever so far away!" said Phil, dolefully. "The beginning of that bend is more than a mile off, I should say."

"Yes, it's a good piece off," said Adam, "and I don't believe we'd better try to make it to-night. The best thing we can do is to camp just here."

At this the boys gave a cheer.

"That's splendid!" said Chap. "I'd rather camp out than go to fifty houses!"

And, casting his traps on the ground, he called on all hands to go and put up the tent.

"You needn't be in such a hurry about the tent," said Adam. "That's the easiest thing we have to do. After awhile me and one of you will

fix up the tarpaulin between a couple of trees back
here, and as it isn't likely to rain, that'll be all
the shelter we'll want. But the first thing to do
is to get supper. Have any of you got fishin'-
lines?"

Each of the boys declared he had one, and
started to get it out of his valise.

"Two'll be enough," said Adam. "One of you
might stay and help me with the fire and things,
while the other two go and fish."

Phœnix agreed to stay and help Adam, while
Phil and Chap got out their lines.

"I was afraid your hooks wouldn't be big
enough," said Adam, taking up their lines; "but
this is a regular deep-sea tackle."

"Yes; my uncle gave us the lines," said Phil.
"He thought we might get some fishing down at
the Breakwater."

"Well, all you got to do," said Adam, "is to go
down to the beach and throw out your lines as fur
as they will go. We'll have to bait at first with a
little piece of meat from the rations the captain
gave us. Of course, you needn't fish if you don't
want to. We've got enough to eat, but I thought
it would seem more to you like real campin' out if
we had a mess of nice hot fish for supper."

"That's so!" cried Chap; "we wouldn't think
of eating that dry stuff while there's fish in the
river."

"That is, if we can coax any of the fish out of the river," remarked Phil.

"Oh, we'll do that easy enough," said Chap. "Get your bait, and come along."

The two boys proceeded a short distance from their proposed camping-ground, and having baited their hooks with some fat and rather gristly beef, they proceeded to throw out their lines; but as they were not used to this kind of fishing, neither of them succeeded in getting his line out into deep water.

Adam had been watching them, and seeing that they were making out badly, he came down to give them what he called "a start." He unwound the whole of each line, and carefully laid it in coils on the sand. Holding the shore end of the line firmly in his left hand, he swung the hook and heavy lead several times above his head, and let it go. The long line flew out its full length, and the lead and bait plunged into deep water. When each of the lines had been thus put out, he went back to his own work.

It was not long before the boys began to have bites, and in a few minutes Chap commenced hauling in his line like a house a-fire. Hand-over-hand he grasped and jerked the cord, throwing it wildly to each side of him as he violently pulled it in. In a moment he drew a fish out of the water, and threw it up high on the sand.

Rushing to it, he picked it up, and held it in the air.

"Look at that!" he cried to Phil. "A splendid fellow! It must be nearly a foot long."

Phœnix and Phil were both interested in the first fish caught in Florida waters, and they ran to look at it. Adam, also, who was picking up driftwood near by, came to see Chap's prize.

"It will do for bait," he said, as he took the fish from the hook.

"Bait!" cried Chap, in amazement. "A big, fat fish like that for bait!"

Adam laughed.

"A fish like that isn't called a big one in these parts, though I s'pose in your waters it would be a pretty good ketch. It's a mullet, and good enough eatin', though it isn't big enough for a meal for us, and I only want to cook one fish."

"All right!" said Chap. "If there are fish big enough for you in this river, I'll catch them."

The mullet was killed, and both lines baited with a large piece of its flesh; for it was food much more attractive to the big fish they wanted, Adam said, than the cold meat they had used before. Phil went farther down the river, and both boys put out their own lines this time, succeeding, after several attempts, in throwing them a considerable distance from the shore.

In less than two minutes Chap felt a tug at his line. He gave a pull, and his first impression was that his hook had caught in something at the bottom, but the jerking of his line soon let him know that there was a fish at the other end of it. Then he began to haul in; but this hauling in was very different from anything he had been accustomed to.

It took all his strength to pull in the line hand-over-hand, and although he was greatly excited, and worked as fast as he could, it came in but slowly. Sometimes the fish pulled back so hard that Chap thought he would be dragged into the water himself; but, digging his heels into the sand, he tugged away manfully.

The line was a stout one, but it cut his hands, and his arms began to ache from the unaccustomed exercise. But he kept bravely on until the head and back of a great fish appeared above the surface of the water.

Wildly excited, he gave a few mad pulls, and then rushing backward, he hauled high up in the sand a flapping, floundering fish, nearly three feet long. It was a handsome creature, dark on the back, but bright yellow beneath.

For a moment Chap gazed on his prize with triumphant delight, and then he gave a shout, which brought Phœnix, and soon after, Adam.

Phœnix was almost as delighted as Chap himself. This was something like fishing. He had never seen a fish like this in his life.

"Now, then," cried Chap to Adam, "what do you say to that? Is that fellow big enough for you?"

"Yes," said Adam, "it's big enough, and it's too big. That's a cavalio, and people eat them when they can't get anything else; but its flesh is pretty coarse, and I couldn't manage to cook a fish that size the way I'm goin' to do it."

"You ought to mention the exact size of fish you want," said Chap, in a disappointed tone, "and then, perhaps, a fellow could catch them for you."

"It is a pity you didn't get something between the two," said Adam; "but you can't expect to hit anything right square the first time. But, hello! here comes the quartermaster, and I believe he's got a blue-fish."

Phil now came running up, carrying a fish nearly as long as his arm. As he came near, he raised the flapping fish, whose tail had been draging in the sand, and gave a shout; but when he saw the magnificent creature, which was still plunging and rolling at the end of the line which Chap held firmly in his hand, his countenance fell.

"What a whopper!" he cried. "Why, mine is nothing to it!"

"No," said Adam, "but yours is a blue-fish,

and we'll have him for supper. Don't be cast down, captain; you'll have plenty of chances yet for blue-fish, bass, and lots of other good fellers. I'll take the hook out of this young elephant of your'n, as he might snap your fingers, and then we'll shove him into the water. He looks lively enough to come to all right when he gets into salt water agen, and there's no use in lettin' fish die here if you ain't goin' to use 'em."

"All right!" said Chap. "I'm captain, and it was my duty to catch the biggest fish, and I've done it. And now the quicker we cook this little fellow for supper, the better, for I'm dreadfully hungry."

The "little fellow," a fish nearly two feet long, was taken in charge by Adam, and carried to the camp-ground, where a large fire was already blazing.

"It was havin' this paper along," said Adam, "that put it into my head to try baked fish for supper."

Having dressed the fish, Adam rolled it in the brown paper, and pushing away a portion of the fire, he scooped out a place in the warm sand and ashes, and covered up the fish therein. Then the fire was built up again, and was allowed to blaze away until Adam thought his fish was done.

When the brown paper was removed, the skin of the blue-fish came off with it, leaving the white flesh perfectly baked and temptingly hot.

There was salt and pepper among their rations, and with the fish and the bread and butter and biscuits, the boys and Adam made a splendid meal, although they had nothing to drink with it but the water from their canteens.

"The way to make a tip-top meal off of fish," said Chap, "is to catch it yourself—or else let some other fellow do it."

CHAPTER V.

CHAP'S ALLIGATOR.

THE preparations for the night were very simple. Adam, whose previous experience in camping and rough life had made him think, before leaving the steamer, of a good many little things that might be useful on a journey such as the one proposed, had brought with him a long, thin rope, something like a clothes-line.

"There's nothin' like havin' plenty of line along," he said, as he fastened one end of this to a low branch of a tree. "It always comes in useful. I'm goin' to hang the tarpaulin on this, and make a tent of it."

"The rope is long enough," said Phœnix.

"Yes," said Adam; "but you can't have a rope too long. The nearest tree that 'twould do to tie it to might be a hundred feet away, don't you see?"

50

There was a suitable tree, however, not a dozen feet from the one just mentioned, and to a low branch of this Adam made his line fast, tying it in a slip-knot, and coiling the slack rope on the ground. This proceeding was made the text of another sermon from the prudent sailor.

"Never cut a line, if you can help it," he said. "Use what you want, and coil away the slack. The time will come when you'll want the longest line you can get."

The tarpaulin was thrown over the low rope, and its edges held out by cords and pegs, which Adam had prepared while the supper was being cooked.

"It'll be pretty close quarters," he said, looking into the little tent, "but you fellers can squeeze into it, and I can sleep outside as well as not. The sand is as dry as a chip, and if you put on your overcoats, and take your carpet-bags for pillows, you'll be just as comfortable as if you was at home in your feather beds."

"A good deal more so, I should think," said Phil, "in mild weather like this."

The boys would not allow Adam to sleep outside. As the tarpaulin was arranged, if there was room enough for three, there was room enough for four. The tent was open at both ends, and they lay in pairs, with their feet inside and their heads near the open ends, so as to get plenty of air.

Adam was soon asleep, but the boys did not

close their eyes for some time. The novelty of
the situation as they thus lay on the soft dry sand,
with the tropical foliage all around them, the
broad river rippling but a short distance away,
and the darkness of this night in an almost foreign
land, relieved only by the flashes of the dying
camp-fire and the bright stars in the clear sky,
kept them awake.

Far off in the river they heard, every now and
then, a dull pounding noise, as if some one were
thumping at the door of a house. This, Adam told
them before he went to sleep, was caused by the
drum-fish, who make these loud sounds as they
swim near the bottom of the river.

Now and then they heard a distant snort or
roar, but from what sort of animal it came they did
not know. They were aware that in the woods of
Florida there were panthers, bears, and wild-cats;
but Adam had told them that in this part of the
country these animals were very shy and seldom
disturbed any one if not disturbed themselves.

After a time Phil and Phœnix fell asleep, but
Chap did not close his eyes. He was an excitable
fellow, and he was thinking what he should do if a
wild beast should invade their camp. There were
no fire-arms in the party, but he thought of several
ways in which four active persons could seize a
wild-cat, for instance, and hold it so that it could
harm no one of them.

After a time the moon rose, and then Chap, lying with his face turned toward the river, was fascinated by the strange beauty of the scene.

While gazing thus, he saw two small animals slowly creeping across the sand and approaching the tent. The sight of them startled him, and he was about to give an alarm, when he suddenly checked himself. These could not be wild-cats, he thought; they were too little and their movements too slow.

As they came nearer and turned their heads toward him, he saw by the now bright rays of the moon that they had light triangular faces, gray bodies, and rat-like tails, and that they were opossums. He had seen these animals in the North, and laughed quietly when he thought they had frightened him. They were evidently after some pieces of fish which lay near the dead ashes of the camp-fire, and were soon making a comfortable meal.

"I never saw such tame creatures," thought Chap. "They must know there are people about."

Then he gave a low, soft whistle. The opossums looked up, but did not move. There was a piece of stick within reach of his hand, and picking it up, he whirled it toward them. They looked up again, but still did not move.

Slowly drawing himself out of the tent so as not to disturb the others, Chap rose to his feet and approached the opossums. One of them turned and ambled slowly to a short distance, but the other stood still.

Chap walked close up to him, but the creature merely arched its back and looked at him.

Picking up a stick which was lying near the ashes, Chap gave the stupid creature a little punch. The opossum merely twisted itself up a little and opened its mouth.

"Upon my word!" said Chap; "if you are not the tamest wild beasts in the world! I don't believe either of you ever saw a man before, and don't know that you ought to be afraid of him. But I'm not going to hurt a non-resistant. You can go ahead and eat your supper, for all I care."

And so he slipped quietly back into the tent, and left the opossums to continue their meal.

It might have been supposed that when Chap did close his eyes, he would sleep longer than the others, but this was not the case. Either because he did not rest well in a new place, or because his mind was disturbed by his responsibilities as captain of the party, he awoke before any of the others. It was broad daylight, and again he slipped out of the tent without disturbing any of his companions.

The opossums were gone, and Chap walked along the water's edge, looking at the hosts of birds which were flying above him. There were gulls and many others which he did not know, and near the other side of the river was a small flock of very large birds, which he supposed must be pelicans.

As he walked round the little clump of trees, under which the tent was pitched, he saw upon the sand, near the water's edge, something which made his heart jump.

It was an alligator, the first Chap had ever seen out of a menagerie. It was about eight feet long, and was lying in the sunshine, with its head toward the water.

Chap stood and gazed at it with mingled amazement and delight. He never thought of fear, for he knew an alligator would not come after him.

Slowly and gradually he came nearer and nearer the strange creature. It did not move. Was it dead? or asleep? He felt sure it was the latter, for it did not look dead. What a splendid thing it was to be so near a live alligator on its native sands! If there were only some way of catching it! That was almost too glorious to think of. If he had a rifle he might shoot it; but that would be nothing. But to catch it alive! The idea fired his soul. He would give anything to capture this fellow, but how could he do it?

He remembered the account that had so pleased him, when he was a boy, of the English captain— Waterton, he thought his name was—who sprang astride of an alligator, and seizing its forepaws, twisted them over its back so that the creature could not walk, nor reach its captor with its jaws or tail.

At first Chap thought that he might possibly do this, but he saw it would be a risky business. The alligator's paws looked very strong, and he might not be able to hold them above its back. Even if it got one paw loose, it might turn round and make things lively.

"If I could only get a rope round the end of his tail," thought Chap, "I could tie him to a tree. That would be simply splendid!"

This plan really looked more feasible than any other. The alligator was lying with his tail turned a little to the left, and the end of it raised slightly from the sand. It might be possible to slip a rope around this without waking the creature; but where was the rope? Chap racked his brain for an instant. Had they a rope?

Then he remembered the line that supported the tent. There was ever so much of it coiled on the sand, it was already fastened to a tree. If the loose length would reach the alligator, and if he could get the end of it around his tail, and the line was strong enough to hold him, he would have him sure.

Wouldn't it be glorious to wake up the other fellows and show them the captive alligator which he had caught all by himself while they were fast asleep?

Slipping off his shoes, he stole softly around to the foot of the tree by the tent where the coil of rope lay. Taking the loose end in his hand, he turned, and slowly crept toward the alligator.

The creature was asleep, and Chap made so little noise as he gradually came near it, that its repose was not disturbed. To his great joy, Chap found that the rope was long enough. When he was almost near enough to touch the tip and of the alligator's tail, he kneeled on one knee, ready to spring up in an instant if the creature should awake, and hesitated for a moment before proceeding to attach the rope.

If he tried to tie it on, the alligator might move before he had time to make a good knot. It would be better to prepare a slip-noose, and put that over the end of his tail. Then when he moved or jerked, he would pull the rope tight.

Chap made a slip-knot and a noose, and, with quickly-beating heart, he leaned forward, and with both hands he gently put the open noose around the alligator's tail.

He did this so cautiously and carefully that the rope did not touch the creature until it was seven or eight inches above the tip of the tail. Then he gently pulled it so as to tighten it.

Almost at the first moment that the rope touched the alligator it gave its tail a little twitch. Chap sprang to his feet and ran backward several yards. Then the alligator raised its head, looked back, and saw him.

Without a moment's hesitation the creature lifted itself on its short legs and made for the river. Chap trembled with the excitement of the moment. Would the noose slip off? Would the rope hold?

The noose did not slip off, it tightened; and in a moment the rope was stretched to its utmost length.

Chap was about to give a shout of triumph, when the alligator, feeling a tug on his tail, became panic-stricken and bolted wildly for the water.

The rope, though not heavy, was a strong one, and it did not break, but the slip-knot around the nearest tree to which it was tied was pulled loose in an instant, and down came the tent on the sleepers beneath it.

Then there was a tremendous jerk on the branch to which the extreme end was tied, and in an instant it was torn from the trunk of the tree.

This branch caught in the end of the tarpaulin, the pegs were jerked out of the sand, and the whole tent was hauled roughly and swiftly over the recumbent Adam and the two boys. The branch got under Phil's head and jerked him into a sitting position almost before it woke him up.

Phœnix thought an earthquake had occurred. In an instant he was enveloped in darkness; then there seemed to be a land slide over his head, and flying bits of wood banged about his ears.

Adam made a grab at the tarpaulin as it swept over him, and held fast to one corner of it. He was instantly jerked about three yards along the sand, and then the branch, to which the end of the rope was tied, slipped under the tarpaulin, and Adam and the tent were left lying together on the ground.

Chap made a wild rush after the branch, but it was pulled into the water before he could reach it. He could see it floating rapidly along the top of the water, as the alligator swam away, and he stood sadly on the bank, watching the disappearance of that branch and his hopes.

Adam, with the two boys, now appeared, half awake and utterly astounded, and anxiously demanded to know what had happened. Never had they been awakened in such a startling style. When Chap explained the state of affairs, Phil and Phœnix burst into a laugh, but Adam looked rather glum.

"You don't mean to say," he exclaimed, "that that 'gator has gone off with all my rope?"

"He's got it all," said Chap; "and I'm sorry now it didn't break, so some of it might have been left. But I tell you what we could do, if we could only get a boat; we could run after that branch—it won't sink, you know—and when we got hold of the rope we might haul the alligator in."

"Haul him in !" cried Adam; "I'd like to see myself hauling a live alligator into a boat, even if we could do it, and had a boat. No, that line is gone for good. He's turned round and chawed it off his tail by this time."

"What did you expect to do with your alligator," asked Phil, "after you had fastened him to a tree? We haven't anything to kill him with, and he would have raged around at the end of his line like a mad bull."

"Perhaps Chap thought he could tame it, and take it along with us," said Phœnix.

"Look here, boys," said Chap, "I don't want any criticisms on this alligator business. If I'd been acting as your captain, and leading you in an alligator hunt, you might say what you pleased when the beast got away; but I was doing this thing in my private capacity, and not as commander of the party, and you fellows have nothing to do with it."

"Haven't we?" cried Phil. "When my head was nearly jerked off, and three or four yards of tent hauled over my face?"

"And I was scared worse than if I had been pulled out of bed with a rake?" said Phœnix.

"Nothin' to do with it!" exclaimed Adam. "When my rope was jerked out of sight and hearin' in a minute, and the tarpaulin would 'a' gone with it, if I hadn't grabbed it? I should think we had something to do with it."

"Perhaps you had," said Chap, as he sat down on the sand to put on his shoes. "But I tell you what it is, fellows," he added, with sparkling eyes, "if we could have tied a live alligator to a tree, it would have been a splendid thing to tell when we got home."

"There is people," said Adam, dryly, "who'd tell a story like that without tyin' a 'gator to a tree."

"But we are not that kind," promptly answered Captain Chap.

"But I guess we won't cry over spilt milk, or lost ropes, either," said Adam; "and the best thing we kin do is to get along to John Brewer's house and see about some breakfast."

"We might catch some more fish," said Chap, "and have breakfast before we started."

"If you kin ketch some coffee," said Adam, "I'll be willin' to talk about breakfast here; but I don't want to make another meal off fish and warm water, if I can help it. John Brewer's house is just the other side of that bend, and we'll be there in half an hour."

The tarpaulin was rolled up, each of the party

picked up his individual traps, and, headed by Chap, they were soon walking along the shore of the river.

When they turned the bend above, they were delighted to see that Adam was right, and that John Brewer's house was really there. It was not much of a house, for it was a frame building, one story high, and containing three or four rooms; but it had an air of human habitation about it which was very welcome to the wanderers. It stood in a small clearing, and John Brewer, a little man, with long, brown hair, which looked as if the wind had been blowing it in several directions during the night, came out of his front door to meet them. Two of his children followed him, and the three others and his wife looked out of a half-opened window.

Mr. Brewer was mildly surprised to see his old acquaintance, Adam, and the three boys, and when he had heard their story, he took a kind but languid interest in the matter, and went into the house to see about getting breakfast.

It was not long before our friends were sitting down to a plentiful meal of coffee, corn bread, and very tough bacon, Mr. Brewer and his family standing at the end of the table and gazing at them as they ate. Some of them would have joined the breakfast-party had there been plates and cups enough.

About half an hour after breakfast, as our friends, with Mr. Brewer and four of the children, were sitting in the shade in front of the house, and Mrs. Brewer and the other child were looking at them behind a half-opened window-shutter, Adam remarked,—

"What I want to know is what chance we have of gettin' up the river to Titusville?"

"How did you expect to get up?" asked Mr. Brewer.

"Well," said Adam, "I thought we might get passage in a mail-boat, if one happened to come along at the right time; and if it didn't, I thought there'd be some boat or other goin' up the river to-day that would take us."

"Well, if them's your kalkerlations," said Mr. Brewer, gently rubbing his knees and looking out over the water, "I don't think you're going to get up at all."

"Not get up at all!" cried the boys; and Adam looked puzzled.

"Well, not for a week or so, anyway," said Mr. Brewer, his eyes still fixed upon the rippling waters. "To be sure, the mail-boat will be along to-day, and she'll stop if she's hailed, but she can't carry you all, and as for other boats, the long and short of it is, there ain't none gone down, and there can't none come up. There was a boat went up yesterday with vegetables from Lake Worth, but she won't be back for a week, and then it'll be a good while before she goes up again. Every boat that's been down the river this month has gone up, and they tell me there ain't nothin' at Jupiter but the little sloop that belongs to the light-house keeper, and she's hauled up to have a new mast put in her."

"Then what are we to do?" asked Phil, anxiously.

"Dunno," said Mr. Brewer.

CHAPTER VI.

THE ROLLING STONE.

THE announcement so placidly made by Mr. John Brewer that it was impossible for our friends to get up the river until some of the sail-boats or small sloops—the only craft which then navigated that stream—should come down and go up again, gave rather a doleful hue to the state of affairs.

Mr. Brewer stated that when a boat came down that far, she generally went all the way to Jupiter Inlet before she returned, and some of the big ones, when they got down there, went outside, and made a trip to Lake Worth, and they would, of course, be still longer coming back.

The spirits of the boys were a good deal depressed, but Adam did not give up his hope that they might get passage on the mail-boat.

"We can stow ourselves somewhere," he said, "and when we get to Fort Capron, we're likely

to find a boat that'll take us the rest of the
way."

But when, an hour after, the mail-boat came in
sight, even Adam's hopes were crushed. It was
not larger than a row-boat, with a small sail, and a
cabin not three feet high, and besides the young
man who sailed her, she already contained two
passengers,—a sportsman who was returning north
and a negro boy. There was no room for the latter to sit in the afterpart of the vessel, and he had
to make himself as comfortable as he could on the
little bit of deck in front of the mast.

It was so obviously plain that four additional
passengers could not get on board that little boat
that the subject was not even broached, Adam con-
fining himself to inquiries in regard to the possi-
bilities of there being other boats down the river
of which Mr. Brewer had not heard. But the
mail-carrier assured him that there were no boats
down there that could come up inside of a week,
and the sportsman declared that he never would
have squeezed himself inside this little tub if there
had been any other chance of his getting up the river.

There was only one relief afforded by the mail-
boat. The boys, anticipating that they might not
be able to go on themselves, had each written a
letter to his family, telling where he was, and
giving a brief history of the state of affairs. Each
letter, written on rumpled stationery supplied by

Mr. Brewer, contained assurances of the perfect safety of the writer, and a request for money to be forwarded to Jacksonville, Florida, which point they hoped to reach in good time.

These, with money for the postage, were given to the carrier, who promised to have them properly mailed at the first post-office on the river.

A telegram was also written and given to the sporting gentleman, who promised to forward it as soon as he reached Sanford, on the St. John's River, this being the nearest point from which telegrams could be sent.

"There, now," said Chap, when the little boat had sailed away, "I feel more comfortable. The folks will know all about us just as soon as if we had gone on ourselves, and that's the main thing; for, as far as I'm concerned, I'm in no particular hurry to get home."

"You don't want to stay here, do you?" asked Phœnix.

"No," said Chap; "but we can tramp along and camp out for a while, till a boat comes by and takes us on. I don't want any better fun than that."

"We can't tramp much farther on this beach," said Phil. "It only reaches about a mile above us, Mr. Brewer says, and tramping and camping for a week or two, with no paths to walk in and nothing to eat, would be pretty tough work."

"We could push back to the sea-shore," said Chap, "and walk along there."

"That might do as far as the walking is concerned," said Phœnix; "but how about the victuals?"

"I'm not quartermaster," said Chap, "I'm captain; and I'll lead you fellows anywhere you want to go."

"That's the way to talk," said Phil; "but it won't do to lead us to any place so far from this house that we can't hear them call at meal-time. We can't live straight along on fish, you know."

A few minutes after this conversation, Adam Guy walked up to Mr. Brewer, who was leaning on the fence of his little garden.

"Look here, John Brewer!" he cried; "what did you mean by sayin' that we couldn't get a boat to go up the river in? In that little creek back there, there's a boat plenty big enough for us. Don't she belong to you?"

"Yes," said Mr. Brewer, "she's mine, but her mast's unshipped, and her mainsail's in the house to be mended."

"Can't we ship the mast and mend the sail?" asked Adam.

"Yes, you might do that," answered Mr. Brewer.

"Well, then," cried Adam, "we're all right!

She doesn't leak, does she? And you'll hire her to us, won't you?"

"Her hull's all right," said Mr. John Brewer, "and I reckon I'd hire her to you."

"And why didn't you tell us about her before?" exclaimed Adam.

"You didn't say anything about my hirin' you a boat," said the other. "If you'd 'a' asked me, I'd 'a' said you could have her."

Adam's shouts soon brought the boys together, and a bargain was speedily concluded with Mr. Brewer, who agreed to hire his boat to our party for a dollar a day.

"That is, till we reach Titusville," said Adam; "but how are we goin' to get her back?"

"Well," said Mr. Brewer, "my brother went up to Enterprise last week, and he'll be comin' back afore long, and it'll suit him fust-rate if you'll leave the boat at Titusville, and then he can come down in her and save payin' his passage on the mail-boat."

"That's a pretty good arrangement for you and your brother," said Chap. "I wonder you didn't think of it before!"

"I didn't want to bother anybody to take a boat up the river jist for my brother," said Mr. Brewer.

Everybody now went gayly to work, Adam mending the sail with true sailor-like skill, and the boys, under Mr. Brewer's direction, and with some of his assistance, getting the mast properly shipped and the boat cleaned out and made ready for her voyage.

She was a well-built little craft, about twenty feet long, and with a small cabin, which would comfortably accommodate four persons. She carried a main-sail and a jib, and was, altogether, very suitable for the purposes of our friends.

By night the boat was ready for the trip, but it was decided to postpone starting until the next morning. All the provisions which Mr. Brewer could spare were purchased, and, although he could not let them have enough to last the three or four days which it would require to reach Titusville, there were places along the river where they could replenish their stores.

Mr. Brewer knew Adam for a good sailor, and had no hesitancy in trusting the boat to his care.

The boys were perfectly delighted at the prospect before them. To sail up the river in a boat which was entirely their own during the voyage was a piece of good fortune they had not dreamed of.

"What is the name of your boat?" asked Chap of Mr. Brewer, as they all sat together after supper.

"Just now she ain't got no name. She used to be called the Jane P., after my first wife; but when she died I painted the name out, and this Mrs. Brewer don't want the boat named after her, because she's afraid she might die too; so, you see, she ain't got no name."

"Well, then," cried Chap, "we can name her ourselves—can't we?"

"Oh, yes," said Mr. Brewer, "you can call her what you please, so long as you don't name her after Mrs. Brewer."

The boys heartily agreed to this restriction, and a variety of names was now proposed; but after a time, the boys concluded that a title suggested by Phœnix was the jolliest and most suitable name for their boat, and they agreed to call her "The Rolling Stone."

"That's a mighty queer name for a boat," said Mr. Brewer. "It seems like it would sink her."

"But you needn't keep it after we've done with her," said Phil.

"I don't think I will," said Mr. Brewer.

And Adam, who had declared the name decidedly un-nautical and with something of an unlucky sound about it, said that after all he reckoned it didn't matter much what the boat's name was, provided they had a good wind.

The next morning, after an early breakfast, provisions and a small keg of fresh water were put aboard; the baggage of the voyagers was safely stowed away; a double-barrelled gun, which had been hired of Mr. Brewer, was hung on a couple of little hooks inside the cabin, with the powder-flask and shot-pouch gracefully dangling beneath it; our party got on board, the sails were run up, and with a parting cheer to Mr. Brewer and three of his children, who stood on the bank of the little creek, and to Mrs. Brewer and the other child, who looked out from behind a half-opened shutter, The Rolling Stone was brought around to the wind, and sailed away on a long tack up the Indian River.

CHAPTER VII.

THE TWO ORPHANS.

THE day was bright and beautiful, there was a fair wind, and The Rolling Stone, bending gently away from the breeze, sailed gayly over the rippling water. Adam was at the helm, and the boys were making themselves comfortable in various parts of the little craft, and enjoying to the utmost the delightful air and the bright sunshine.

"I tell you what it is, boys!" cried Chap, who was stretched at full length on top of the little cabin, relying on Adam to give him notice when the boat was to be put about and the boom would swing around, "do you know I'd be as happy as a king if I felt sure our folks wouldn't be worried about us?"

"I don't think we need worry about them," said Phil, "for that hunting man said he'd be at Sanford before long, and then all our folks will hear from us just as quick as the telegraph can carry word to them."

"There's a comfort in that," said Chap.

And Phœnix suggested that they might as well be as jolly as the law allowed.

Adam made no remark upon the subject. He knew very well that it might take the sportsman a week, or perhaps longer, to reach the point from which he was to send the telegram he carried, but he wisely concluded that it would be of no use to dampen the spirits of his young companions, and that it would be better for all hands that they should be lively and cheerful.

"Look here," he said, "you boys can be happy as kings, if you like, but you needn't think you're goin' to be lazy. I'm goin' to teach you how to lend a hand to the sails, and make yourselves useful aboard ship."

"Lazy?" cried Chap. "Rolling stones are never lazy. Boys," he exclaimed, struck by a sudden inspiration, "let's call ourselves 'The Rolling Stones.' It's as good a name for us as it is for the boat, and we expect to roll on till we get home."

"Agreed!" cried Phil and Phœnix.

And the name was adopted.

They sailed all day, eating a slight lunch about noon, and it was decided to anchor toward the close of the afternoon, and eat their evening meal on shore.

The boys were anxious to have wild duck for supper, and they shot three or four of these birds, Adam skilfully steering the boat so close to the floating game that it could easily be picked up. Some fish were caught, and a fine fire was kindled on the beach.

Cups, saucers, and a few cooking utensils had been procured from Mr. Brewer, and with roast duck, fish, some bacon, corn-bread and biscuit, and hot coffee, the party made an excellent meal.

They sat round the camp-fire on the river bank until it was nearly dark, and then they went on board The Rolling Stone, and having tied her up securely, and made all things tight and right, they stowed themselves away in the cabin, which was divided into two compartments by the centre-board, and were soon asleep on the plain but sufficient bedding with which Mr. Brewer had furnished the boat.

The next morning there was no wind at all. The surface of the river was as smooth as glass, and was only rippled by the water-fowl, which rose from or settled down upon it, or by the schools of little fish, which occasionally sprang a short distance out of the water, and fell pattering back like a shower of gravel-stones.

" It's no use to set sail till the wind rises," said Adam; "so we might as well try to make ourselves contented on shore for a while. About ten or eleven o'clock p'rhaps we'll have a breeze."

"All right!" said Chap. "We can pole the boat out into deep water and fish."

"Yes," said Adam, "you boys can do that, if you like; but I think I'll take the gun and go into the woods, and see if I can't find some game. I noticed this mornin' a kind o' path back there which looked to me like a bear track. I've seen bear tracks afore, and, though I ain't certain about this one, I think I'll foller it up a little way."

"Good!" cried Phil; "and I'll go with you."

Adam hesitated.

"I dunno about that," he said. "If we was to meet a bear, you wouldn't have any gun, and you might feel sort o' helpless. I'd tell you to take the gun and go by yourself, but I guess I know more about the ways of these wild critters than you do."

"I don't want to go alone," said Phil, "and I'm not afraid to go without a gun. There are two barrels there, and you can use one for me and one for yourself."

"Very well," said Adam, "you can come. This shot-gun isn't the right thing to take along if we expect to meet bears, but I'll put half a dozen buckshot into each barrel, and I guess that'll do for anything we get a crack at."

Phœnix would have been glad to go with Phil and Adam, but in that case Chap would have been left alone; and, besides, it would not do to make a bear-hunting party too large. So he got out his fishing-lines, and helped Chap pole the boat into deeper water, where they anchored her, and set comfortably to work to fish. The sport was not very exciting, for the large fish are only found in certain portions of the river, but the biting was lively, and the fish they hauled up were a good deal larger than those they used to catch at home.

Adam and Phil made their way slowly along a path which the former had taken to be a bear track. Sometimes they got through the under-brush quite easily, and then, again, it would be very difficult and unpleasant to push through the thorny shrubbery and under low-hanging branches of small trees.

"If we went on all-fours, like a bear," said Adam, "it would be easy enough; but as we don't, we've got to make the best of it."

They made the best of it for some time, occasionally losing the track, and then, finding it again, or supposing they had found it, they would bravely press forward.

At last, to their great relief, they came to a place where the way was much more open; the bed of a very small stream, now dry, wound before them through the forest, and, as it was free from underbrush, it made a very convenient pathway.

There was nothing in the appearance of this dry bed to indicate that a bear had been in the habit of walking in it; but, as it made a very good passage through the forest for a man and a boy, Phil and Adam cheerfully took their way up the stream.

It did not matter much whether they saw a bear or not; for, if they did catch sight of one, Adam very much doubted if he could get it within range of a shot-gun. But they were both fond of the woods, and were glad to explore a semi-tropical forest like this.

Adam was a hunter, as well as a sailor, for his adventurous experiences had been both on land and sea.

On either side of them was a mass of vines and bushes, out of which the shorter or cabbage palmettos arose, wherever they could find room to spread their long and drooping leaf-stalks, which not only grew from their crests, but sprang out of the sides of their trunks, while, high above was the vast and impenetrable canopy of the leaves of the tall palmettos, each umbrella-like tuft supported by a long and slender stem.

The forest thus appeared to be covered by a roof of green, held up by innumerable gray columns of pillars.

Sometimes the monotony of the palmettos was

broken by great live-oak trees, which reached high
into the air, and whose massive branches, often
curiously grotesque and crooked, bore not only
their own bright and glossy leaves, but were covered throughout their length with vines and various fern-like growths, while from the lower part
of these limbs, and from the trunks and branches
of many other trees, hung long and graceful
festoons of the silver-gray Spanish moss.

The bark of many of the palmetto trunks was
relieved by splotches of bright red, and here and
there, sometimes on dead trees and sometimes on
living ones, there were air-plants, their roots fastened in the dry wood, and their long, bending
leaves stretching out into the air for the nu-
triment which most plants draw up from the
earth.

Phil was greatly interested in all these things,
and Adam gazed about him with much satisfaction, although he had often walked in such woods
before. He had been so long on ships and steamboats that this woodland ramble was a pleasant
change.

Phil stopped to cut some of the red patches of
bark from a palmetto near him, hoping to be able
to carry the pieces home to show as curiosities, and
thus his companion had got some distance ahead
of him.

Adam was walking quietly along, when suddenly he heard, from a clump of thick bushes to his right, a low but very peculiar sound. It was a series of little whimpers and sniffs, that would not have been heard at all if the woods had not been so quiet.

Instantly Adam stopped. He was sure he recognized that sound. Turning to the point whence it came, he peered earnestly into the shrubbery. Just above a low, heavy bush, not a dozen feet away from him, he saw the top of a round, black head, and a pair of glistening eyes.

Without hesitating for a moment, he cocked both barrels of his gun, and taking a quick aim just above the eyes he saw before him, he pulled both triggers. A loud report rang through the forest, and the head disappeared.

Phil, astounded by the discharge of the gun, started to run toward Adam, but the latter waved him back, and retreating a short distance, began rapidly reloading.

When this was done, he waited a few minutes, and then, closely followed by Phil, he approached the bush at which he had fired.

Hearing nothing but the little whimpers which had before attracted his attention, he cautiously made his way around the bush, his gun cocked and ready for instant use.

But there was no occasion to use it. Upon the ground lay a large she-bear, dead, with twelve

Adam tucking the other under his left arm.

buckshot in her brain. In a slightly-hollowed place in the ground behind her were two young bears, about a foot long, round and fat, and rolling and pawing each other, while they continually sniffed and whimpered as if they wanted something, but did not know what it was.

Phil gave a shout of triumph when he hurried up behind Adam and saw the dead bear.

"Why, this is glorious!" he cried. "Who could have thought you would have shot a real wild bear? Are you sure it's dead?"

"Oh, yes," said Adam, cautiously punching the animal with the end of the gun; "bears don't play 'possum. I put both loads into her head. And I didn't do it any too soon, either. In two seconds more she'd a' been out after me."

"Can't we skin her?" cried Phil. "It would be a splendid thing to take home a bear-skin that we got ourselves."

"I'd like well enough to have the skin," said Adam, "but I ain't goin' to stop to take it off. If the old he-bear comes home while we are here, he'll make it hot for us. Just you pick up one of them young cubs, and I'll take the other, and the quicker we're off the better."

Phil had been so delighted at seeing the dead bear that he had scarcely noticed the young ones, but he now picked up one of them, while Adam, tucking the other under his left arm, hastily led

f

the way to the bed of the stream, down which they hurried as fast as they could go.

When Phil and Adam reached the point where they left the bed of the stream, which here turned to the south, and began to force their way through the bushes and vines, and over the uneven ground, they went more slowly.

To push through and under the tangled maze on each side of the barely-discernible track, to hold securely the struggling cub which each of them carried, and to keep an ear open all the time for the approach of an enraged bear, which might be in pursuit of them, was as much as they could do.

CHAPTER VIII.

"CAPTAIN OF HIMSELF."

CAPTAIN CHAP and Treasurer Phœnix had a very good time fishing, and before long they had caught many more fish than they thought would be needed for that night's supper. They were not at all sure that everything they had taken was good to eat, but they thought that Adam would be able to pick out of the catch enough for a meal. They had no bluefish or bass, for this was not a part of the river where these were to be found, nor did Chap have an opportunity to exercise his strength in hauling in another powerful cavalio.

After a time Chap wound up his line.

"It's no use catching any more fish," he said. "We have enough of them now, and we might as well pole the boat ashore, and wash off this forward deck. But before we do that, I'm going to take a swim."

"That would be a good idea," said Phœnix. "It's as warm down in this part of the world as if it was summer-time, and the water looks so nice and clear I feel as if I'd like to jump into it."

Both boys now began to undress, but Chap was ready first, and standing on the top of the little cabin he made a dive into the water. He soon rose again to the surface, and swimming around in a small circle, returned to the boat.

"You'd better take care how you dive," he said to Phœnix, reaching up as he spoke and taking hold of the side of the boat. "The bottom is horrid. It's all covered with oysters, and it won't do to get any of the water in your mouth, for it's salt."

"Why, didn't you know that?" said Phœnix, who was not quite ready to go in. "This river is really only an arm of the sea, and all those big fish we caught the other day came in from the ocean."

"Yes, I remember Adam's telling about it," said Chap, "but I forgot it. I don't believe I care to swim in such water as this. It isn't like the ocean, and it isn't like the real, honest river. The water isn't very deep out here, but it seemed sort of scary to me when I went down."

"I guess that's because of the queer things you know are in the river," suggested Phœnix.

"I shouldn't wonder if that was it," said Chap.

Just at this moment a sound was heard in the river that made the boys jump. It was the noise of something rushing through the water, and, looking around, they saw part of the back and tail of a great fish, which was surging along at a tremendous rate toward the boat.

Chap instinctively pulled himself up by his hands, and Phœnix made a frenzied clutch at his arm and jerked him out of the water and over the side of the boat before Chap knew what he intended to do.

The fish swept within ten feet of them, and then making a turn, it seemed to shake itself as if with disappointment and anger, and, dashing along like a steamboat for a short distance, it raised its tail in the air and disappeared.

"What was that thing?" asked Chap, as soon as he could find voice to speak.

"Can't say," answered Phœnix, his face still pale, "unless it was a shark."

"It couldn't be that," returned Chap. "It must have been a porpoise, or something of that kind."

"Porpoises don't chase people," said Phœnix, "and that creature came after you, Chap. He must have seen you when you made your dive, and it's lucky for you that he didn't start sooner."

"That's so," said Chap. "Let's pull up the anchor and pole her ashore. No more swimming in these waters for me!"

The boys quickly dressed themselves and hauled on the long anchor rope until they had pulled the boat into water where they could reach the bottom with their pole. Then pushing her in, they made her fast to the shore, and went to work to gather up their fish and make things clean and tidy.

While they were thus engaged, Phil and Adam, hot and flushed, made their appearance from the woods. The astonishment of Chap and Phœnix when their companions ran to them and proudly held up the little bears is not to be described.

"Isn't this something like a bear-hunt?" cried Phil. "Killed an old one, and carried off these youngsters. To be sure, Adam did it all, but I gave him moral support."

Chap and Phœnix now loudly demanded a full account of the adventures of the others, and when these had been told and the little bears had been admired and patted and finally stowed away in an old box, which was lined with a blanket from one of the beds, Chap exhibited the fish he and Phœnix had caught, and told of the big fellow they had seen in the water.

"You don't mean to say you went in to swim?" exclaimed Adam. "I never thought of your doin' a thing like that when I left you. Why, do you know you were in a great deal more danger than we were, even if the old man-bear had got after us? That big fish you saw was a shark, and if it had come along a little sooner, it would a' taken off one of your legs as like as not. This is a very good river, but it wasn't made for white folks to swim in—at least, not in these parts. There are plenty of sharks here, and I'm not sure but what you might tempt a 'gator, if you were very anxious to get bit."

"Do you know," said Chap, in a very impressive way, "that I never thought that there were sharks in this river, and that I totally, absolutely, and utterly forgot alligators?"

"Sharks!" exclaimed Adam, looking at the fish the boys had caught. "Why, you ought to have known they were in the river, for here you've got one!"

"A shark!" cried all the boys together, as they clustered around the pile of fish.

"Yes," said Adam, pointing to a fish about a foot and a half long, with a smooth skin and a large flat-topped head; "this is a young shark."

"Upon my word," cried Chap, "we hadn't the least idea of that! We thought the thing was a big cat-fish. We noticed it hadn't any feelers on its mouth, but we supposed cat-fish might be different down here from those we're used to. We had lots of trouble in getting the hook out of its mouth."

"It's a lucky thing you didn't get your fingers

into those jaws," said Adam, "for you might never have got them out again."

"Gentlemen," cried Chap, throwing one arm into the air, "it's time we got away from this place. For all we know, there's a savage bear raging through the woods after some of us, and out there in the river there's an exasperated shark waiting till one of the party is foolish enough to go in to swim or accidentally tumbles overboard. Let's up sail and be off!"

"Well," said Adam, "as there's a good breeze gettin' up from the sou'east, that's about the best thing we can do, even if we don't take into account bears and sharks."

As soon as they were fairly under way, Adam gave the tiller to one of the boys, and set about taking care of his young bears. A small quantity of condensed milk in tin cans had been purchased of Mr. Brewer, and some of this, mixed with water, was fed to the cubs. They were very hungry, and soon lapped it up eagerly.

"It seems like a cruel thing," said Chap, "to break up a family in that manner."

"Well," replied Adam, "the only way bears can be made of any good to anybody is to kill 'em or carry 'em off for shows. If people didn't do that, there'd better be no bears. Now, if I kin keep these young ones alive, and git 'em up North, I kin sell 'em to some menagerie man or show-keeper for a nice little lot of money. Baby bears ain't common in shows, and these are as cute little creatures as I ever see."

The breeze which had arisen did not prove to be very strong, and the progress of The Rolling Stone was slow. After a time the wind gradually changed its direction, and there sprung up one of those sudden squalls which were frequent on the Indian River. The wind blew a hurricane, the surface of the river was covered with tossing waves, and The Rolling Stone would probably have rolled entirely over if Adam had not noticed the approach of the wind-storm and taken quick precautions. The boat was laid with her head to the gale, and both sails were rapidly lowered, and when the little bears had been carefully wrapped up and tucked in, so that they would not take cold, there was nothing to do but to lie to till the storm had passed over.

Then, in the afternoon, the wind got around to the northeast, which was almost dead ahead. Adam was obliged to tack backward and forward all the afternoon. The boys became rather tired of doing so much sailing and making so little progress, and when the boat had gradually worked its way about a mile above a small river, which flowed into the Indian River from the west, everybody was glad to land at a convenient place on the west side of the river and make the evening fire.

The next morning, the wind blew more strongly from the north, and, what was worse, there was not a drop of milk left for the little bears.

"There's a store about fifteen miles above this place," said Adam; "but these cubs will starve before we kin beat up there agin this wind. They take a lot o' feedin', and they're nearly famished now. But back from the river, about a mile and a half up, there's a man who has a little orange-grove. I was there once, and I know he keeps a lot of supplies on hand. I'll walk over there and see if I can't get some milk."

Soon after Adam had started, Phil said he thought he would take the gun and go into the woods, and see if he could not find some game. He did not intend to look for any bears, but he thought he might find something smaller.

"I'd like to go along," said Phœnix, "if it wasn't that somebody has got to take care of the boat and things, and I don't want to leave Chap alone."

"Nobody need trouble himself about me," said Chap; "you go along, and I'll stay here and fish. I made up my mind to do that as soon as Adam said he was going."

"All right," said Phil; "but mind you don't go in to swim."

"You needn't be afraid of that!" cried Chap, as his two companions walked away. "I expect the fish here are not at all like those we caught before," he said to himself, as he cut up some pieces of bait. "They seem to be different at every place we stop."

Chap was a strange fellow. He liked his friends, and he was fond of company, but he was even more fond of entirely independent action.

"Now, then," he said to himself, "I can go ahead and fish just as I please. I'm not quite sure that I'm always captain of this party, but one thing is certain, I can be captain of myself."

CHAPTER IX.

FRIENDS AND ENEMIES.

CHAP began his independent operations by poling The Rolling Stone to some distance from the shore. Then dropping the anchor and letting out the rope, he pushed his boat out as long as his pole would touch bottom.

There was not much current, but the wind blew the boat inland, so that Chap found that he would have to be continually pushing her out if he wished to keep her in water deep enough for fishing.

He was afraid to go out where he could not touch bottom with his pole, for the wind was strong, and he did not know what would happen if he tried to sail her.

So, at last, he gave up fishing and poled back to shore. Putting away his fishing tackle, he began to try to comfort the little bears, who were whining and whimpering and tumbling over each other, showing the greatest distress at being obliged to wait for their breakfast.

While thus engaged, there came down the river a dirty little boat, with a dirty little sail, in the stern of which sat two very untidy young men.

When it was within a hundred yards of The Rolling Stone, this boat, the approach of which Chap had not noticed, was run ashore, and the two untidy young men, each carrying a gun, came walking down the narrow beach.

When they were near the boat, Chap heard them, and looking up, was very much surprised to see these strangers. They saluted Chap in a friendly way, and as The Rolling Stone was near the shore, they stepped on board, and sitting down, began to talk to him.

The untidy young men asked Chap a great many questions, all of which he answered freely.

"So you're in a great hurry to get North?" said one of them.

"Oh, yes," said Chap. "You see, our friends don't know where we are, and we wouldn't stop anywhere, if we didn't have to."

"And the rest of the party has gone off and left you here by yourself," said the other. "We was a-wonderin' as we was comin' down what you was doin' here on the boat."

"I tried to fish," said Chap, "but I couldn't keep her out."

"If you fellers want to git up the river in a hurry, you ought to have a smaller boat that'll sail ag'in the wind better'n this one. Now we've got a little boat up there that we want to send back to Titusville, and you've got one you want to send back to John Brewer. If you say so, we'll trade, and that'll suit all parties."

"Oh, we wouldn't think of that," said Chap, rather contemptuously, looking up at the craft they had left. "Your boat is entirely too small for us, and this suits us first-rate. It's a regular little yacht."

"Yes," said the other, looking around him, "she's a mighty comfortable boat."

After examining the little bears, and asking a few more questions, the two young men stepped ashore and walked up to their own boat.

Chap thought they were going to re-embark, but this they did not do. They loaded themselves with some pouches and flasks, a basket containing canned food of various kinds, a bag of flour, and a few articles of wearing apparel.

These things they brought down to The Rolling Stone, and, much to Chap's surprise, they put them all aboard.

"What are you about?" cried our friend, springing to his feet.

"We're goin' to trade boats," said one of the young men, as he stepped on board.

"No, you are not!" cried Chap, in great excitement.

And then, at the top of his voice, he gave a wild shout, hoping that Adam or the boys might hear him.

"Push her off!" said the young man on board to the one on shore.

And in a moment The Rolling Stone was floating in one or two feet of water.

The other young man now scrambled on deck, and, having pulled the anchor on board, he came aft, where Chap was already engaged in endeavoring to put his companion overboard.

Both men now threw themselves on Chap, and, in a very short time, that unfortunate fellow was floundering in the shallow water.

Rising to his feet, he made a rush toward the boat, and would have boarded her had not the muzzle of a shot-gun been pointed at his head.

"Just you stay where you are," said the young man with the gun, as the other seized the pole and pushed The Rolling Stone out into deep water. "If you hadn't hollered for your fellers we'd 'a' put some of your things ashore, but we haven't time for that now. Good-by."

And putting down his gun, the speaker took the tiller, while his companion hauled up the mainsail, and in about a minute The Rolling Stone was scudding down the river before a strong north wind.

At first Chap stood bewildered. His mind could scarcely comprehend the fact that there were two men in the world who would do the thing that these young men had just done. To throw him out of his own boat, and make off with it before his eyes! Could it all be real?

But he did not long stand still. His active nature made it necessary for him to do something. If he had had a gun he would have fired after the rascals, but as it was he could do absolutely nothing by himself, and the first thing to be thought of now was to let the others know what had happened.

Giving a last look at the retreating boat, he saw that one of the young men was pouring what appeared to be milk in a tin basin. The villains knew that the bears were hungry, and as they had milk with them, they evidently intended to feed them and bring them up as their own.

Was there ever such unparalleled impudence? The sight made his blood boil, and he involuntarily shook his fist at the retreating boat.

There was a rough path or narrow roadway which ran through the woods in the direction in which Adam had gone, and along this path Chap now ran at the top of his speed. The boys had also gone this way, and he thought he must soon overtake some of his party.

It happened, however, as it has happened so often before to many a traveller, that Chap soon came to a point where there were two diverging paths, and he did not know which was the one that Adam had taken.

He stopped for about a quarter of a minute to consider, and then, like many another unfortunate traveller, he took the wrong path.

Away he dashed along the track which led to the left, stopping every now and then to shout at the top of his voice. At last his breath began to fail him, and then he rested for a time.

As soon as he had recovered a little, he shouted and shouted again, but no answering shout came back to him, and then he started off again. He did not run now, but he walked rapidly.

If he kept on, he thought, he must soon reach the house to which Adam had gone, but he walked and walked and walked until he felt sure he must have gone two or three miles; but then distances are not judged very accurately in wild places such as this, and Adam might have been mistaken in supposing the house was only a mile and a half away.

This path certainly led somewhere, and he would keep on a little while longer. If he did not soon come to a house, he would turn back.

He did not soon come to a house, and he sat down on a fallen tree to rest. As he sat there, he felt very badly about the matter. As it had so happened that he had not found Adam and the boys, he felt that it would have been better if he had remained by the river. The others had probably arrived there by this time, and when he should get back and tell them what had happened, they would all feel that a great deal of valuable time had been lost by his running away into the woods. He was tired, and hungry, too, and the thought struck him that he did not know how they were going to get anything to eat, unless they all went to the house of which Adam had spoken.

"I'm glad the scoundrels did not run away with Phœnix's money," he thought.

And that was the only ray of comfort that seemed to shine across his present miserable existence.

And yet he did not blame himself for what had happened. Perhaps he ought not to have come so far into the woods, but he had done it for the best.

He now arose, and as he did so he looked along a portion of the path which stretched in an almost straight line before him, and at the end of the little vista which it made, he saw some blue and curling smoke.

" Hurrah !" he cried. " A house is just ahead ! Why on earth was I so foolish as to stop here?" and so saying, he hurried along the path.

When he arrived at the place where he saw the smoke, he found no house, but in a little open space in the woods there was a fire on the ground, and hanging from a branch of a tree above the fire was a covered tin vessel, very much blackened by smoke, in which something seemed to be simmering.

Chap stopped and looked at the fire. As he did so two men arose from the foot of a tree and came toward him. As soon as Chap looked at these men he knew they were Indians.

Chap had seen Indians before in the city near which he lived, but these were on exhibition, and were dressed in all the paraphernalia of blankets, leggings, feathers, and dangling ornaments, which are generally supposed to make up the ordinary costume of the American Indian; but he had never seen the red man in his native wilds, and the dress of these Indians surprised him almost as much as their appearance on the spot. They had copper-colored faces, high cheek-bones, jet-black hair, and wore moccasins, and these were the only points of resemblance between them and the traditional Indian.

They each wore a blue-flannel shirt, a pair of thick cotton trousers, and a dilapidated felt hat.

One of them carried a powder-horn and a buckskin bullet-pouch, and against the tree, beneath which they had been sitting, there leaned a rifle.

As the Indians approached, one of them held out his hand. Chap had not made up his mind whether to be relieved or frightened when he saw the Indians, but he took the tawny hand that was offered him, and gave it a shake. There seemed to be nothing else to do.

CHAPTER X.

PHIL'S UNCLE AND CHAP'S SISTER.

WE must now return for a time to Hyson Hall and its neighborhood, where the families of our three young friends were naturally much disturbed at their long-continued absence. On the morning of the day which Chap Webster had fixed for his return from the Breakwater, Mr. Godfrey Berkeley, Phil's uncle, rode over to the Webster place, and found Chap's mother already wondering what train the boys would come up in.

"Now, Mrs. Webster," said Mr. Godfrey, "don't you expect them by any train to-day. When boys start off on an expedition like that, they cannot fix a date for their return. It is impossible for them to know exactly how long it will take to get to the Breakwater; how many delays will occur while there and on their return. I do not expect them until to-morrow, or perhaps the day after."

These very sensible remarks comforted Mrs. Webster for the time being, but when two more days passed, and her son did not return, she became greatly troubled. Mr. Poole, the father of Phœnix, also sent over to Hyson Hall to know if Mr. Berkeley had heard anything from the boys. Mr. Godfrey himself began to think it was quite time that the young fellows had returned, or made some report of their doings. If they had been delayed at the Breakwater, they should have telegraphed.

While he was considering this matter, and blaming Phil a good deal for his negligence, a messenger came to him from the city, sent by one of the members of the tug-boat company, with whom he was acquainted, telling him how the boat had gone to sea and had never returned, and begging him to break the matter as well as he could to the Webster and Poole families.

Poor Mr. Godfrey had grief enough of his own when he heard this intelligence, but he did not give up hope, and hurried away to do what he could to help and encourage his afflicted neighbors.

The Poole family were very willing to listen to Mr. Berkeley's hopeful words, and promised to keep up good hearts until they could hear from him again, and even Mrs. Webster, although terribly shocked, did not entirely despair. There never was a man who could put a brighter side to dreary things than Mr. Godfrey Berkeley.

"But I shall die upon the spot," she said, "if something is not done. If I can know that somebody is doing something, I can wait in hope; but if we are to sit here with our hands folded, I shall go crazy. I should start off this minute myself if I knew what to do or where to go, and if there were not so many things that make it almost impossible for me to leave home just now."

Mr. Godfrey assured her that something was to be done instantly, for he was going to start for the city by the very next train; thereupon, Helen, Chap's only sister, who was even more grieved by the dreadful news than her mother, although she did not say so much about it, begged that she might go with Mr. Godfrey.

"I want to hear any news as soon as it comes," she said. "I don't think I can sit still here and wait. And then, if anything is heard from them, Mr. Godfrey may want to stay down in the city, and I can come up and tell you. That will be ever so much better than letters and telegrams."

Mr. Webster was absent in the West, and as Mrs. Webster thought it very proper that some of the family should do something in the matter, she gave Helen permission to accompany Mr. Berkeley, who was very glad to have for a companion this sensible and courageous girl.

In the city they heard the full particulars of the occurrence as far as they were known.

"Has nothing been heard of the vessel which the tug-boat went out to offer to bring in?" asked Mr. Godfrey Berkeley.

"She never came into the Breakwater at all," was the answer. "She must have concluded to lie-to that night, for the wind was dead against her. She was the Cygnet, bound to Norfolk, Virginia, and we heard yesterday that she was spoken the next day by a coasting vessel coming North. The gale had pretty well gone down by that time, and she'd rigged up a jury-mast, and was making her way to her port with a fair wind."

"Mr. Godfrey," said Helen, "who had been listening attentively, "don't you suppose that ship might have picked up the people on the tug-boat if they were wrecked? Perhaps Chap and the others are on board of her now."

"I am afraid there is not much hope in that direction," said the agent of the company, "for the tug and the disabled schooner do not appear to have had anything to do with each other. Our belief is that the tug-boat was driven out to sea by the storm, on account of some of her machinery getting out of order, and that the persons on board were probably picked up by some passing vessel, from which we may hear at any day."

"But I think," persisted Helen, "that we ought

not to wait for that. I believe that we ought to go to Norfolk and meet that one-masted schooner. If Chap and the other boys are on board, I'd like to be there when they come in."

Mr. Berkeley had been quietly thinking about the matter, and although he was very much afraid that there was little reason for supposing that his dear Phil and the other boys were on board the Cygnet, still he felt that nothing should be left undone, and that even this little ray of hope should not be abandoned, and he therefore determined to go to Norfolk, and as Helen plead so earnestly to go with him, he agreed to take her.

She asserted that her valise contained everything she needed, and he assumed the responsibility of taking her upon this trip, feeling sure that nothing would satisfy Mrs. Webster so much as to know that something was still being done. He therefore telegraphed to Boontown, and he and Helen set off for Norfolk as soon as possible.

When they reached Norfolk, the Cygnet had not yet come in. Her passage down the coast had probably been very slow, and she might have been also delayed by additional accidents to her sailing-gear, which, from all accounts, must have been in a very bad condition.

Mr. Godfrey and the young girl walked about the piers and wharves all the afternoon, and as night approached, and no Cygnet had come in,

Helen went back to the hotel with a fear that the boys had suffered a second shipwreck.

But early in the morning, word was brought to Mr. Berkeley that the disabled Cygnet lay in the Roads, and it was not long before he and Helen were being rapidly rowed out to the schooner.

But when they went on board, they saw no Chap, no Phil, no Phœnix. The boys had never been on the vessel.

Poor Helen sank down on something, she knew not what it was, and covered her face with her hands, but in a few minutes afterward Mr. Godfrey stood before her, and put his hand on her head.

"Helen!" he cried, "look up. I have splendid news!"

Helen gave a start, and looking at Mr. Berkeley, she saw that his eyes were sparkling, and that his face was glowing with delight.

"Just think of it, Helen!" he cried. "The captain here tells me that the next morning after the tug-boat came out to meet him, he saw her, with his glass, tossing about on the waves a long way off. He knew she must have been blown out to sea by the storm, and he kept watch on her. She was so far away that the people on board of her could not have seen his vessel if they had not a good ship's glass. He was sure she was disabled, and would have gone to her assistance if he had not been disabled himself. But now, hear this—this is the splendid part. Some time afterward, he saw a steamship come along, and as he kept his glass on the spot he saw the steamer lie-to and take people off the tug-boat. Of course, she took everybody. And then she started on her way South. He says he is quite sure she is a Savannah steamer.

"Oh, Mr. Godfrey," cried Helen, clapping her hands, "this is glorious! Let's go straight to Savannah!"

"Why, you madcap girl," laughed Mr. Berkeley, "I believe you would follow those fellows all round the world!"

"Indeed I would," said Helen, "if I could only be sure of meeting dear Chap at last!"

When they went back to the hotel, Mr. Berkeley actually considered this plan of going to Savannah. He calculated that the steamer should have arrived at that port some days before, and if the boys were there, they were probably in trouble, for, otherwise, they certainly should have been heard from.

He could not imagine why they had not telegraphed or written. His joy, therefore, at the news given him by the captain of the Cygnet, was much dampened after this careful consideration of the case. At any rate, he determined to go to Savannah. If the steamer was really bound there, the boys ought to be looked after, and he felt, as well as Mrs. Webster, that something ought to be doing until they were found.

Of course, he had to take Helen with him, as he could not send her home alone, and having telegraphed the Cygnet's news to Boontown, the two started for Savannah that afternoon.

When they reached that city, Mr. Berkeley made diligent inquiries in regard to the arrival of three shipwrecked boys, but he heard that only two steamers had come in within a week, and that neither of these had fallen in with a disabled tug-boat.

When even his stout heart was beginning to despair, and poor Helen looked as if she had been ill for a month, there came a telegram from Boontown. It was from Mr. Welford, a banker of that place, and a friend of Mr. Berkeley's, to whom the telegram had been addressed which the boys had forwarded by the sportsman they had met on the Indian River.

Mr. Welford lived in the town, and a telegram sent to him would be immediately delivered, and the boys knew he would lose no time in notifying their families.

The telegram now received from Mr. Welford informed Mr. Godfrey Berkeley that the boys were on the Indian River, Florida, and were coming North as fast as possible.

This news made the world seem like a different

place to Phil's uncle and Chap's sister. This was something real and tangible.

"It seems as if we knew just where the boys were," cried Helen.

"Yes," said Mr. Godfrey, laughing, "we might take the map, and almost point out the exact spot where they ought to be by this time; but, most probably, we would make a mistake, and we won't do it. It is enough to know that they are in Florida, and we shall probably see them soon."

"Shall we wait here for them?" said Helen.

"I have not made up my mind about that," replied Mr. Berkeley.

But before he made up his mind a telegram came from Mrs. Webster, which read thus:

"Please go and meet my boy. He has not a cent, and scarcely any clothes."

"All right," said Mr. Berkeley, when this characteristic message had been read and considered. "I shall be very glad to take a trip into summer land, for it is getting very bleak and cold up our way. Of course, your mother means that I shall take you with me, Miss Helen, and it will do you good, for if ever a girl needed to have plumpness and rosiness brought back to her cheeks, you do. The boys are bound to come down the St. John's River to Jacksonville, and we can't miss them."

And so the two started for Florida.

"Won't they be surprised when they see us?" said Helen, when she and Mr. Godfrey had taken their seats in the car.

"I hope so," said Mr. Godfrey. "Half our pleasure will be lost if we don't astonish them."

CHAPTER XI.

TWO EXPEDITIONS.

"Come from the river?" said the Indian who had shaken hands with Chap. "Been fishin'? Where's the rest of 'em?"

The very fair English which this Indian spoke was a new surprise to Chap, and for an instant he wondered how the man knew there were any more of them; but as any one might reasonably suppose that a young fellow like himself would not come into this part of the country alone, the question seemed sensible enough. The other Indian now came up, and, without saying anything, seemed very anxious to hear what should be said.

Chap then briefly related his story. For some reason which he could not explain he had for these Indians a feeling very different from that with which, from the very first, he had regarded the untidy young men. To be sure, he had answered their

111

questions, for there seemed to be no good reason for refusing; but he had felt all along that they were unpleasant companions, and had hoped they would soon go away. But these Indians seemed to have honest faces, and to take a friendly interest in what he told them.

When he related how the boat had been stolen from him, the Indians looked at each other, and each of them gave a grunt.

"Big thieves! big thieves!" said one. "Come down on river and steal boat. Very bad thieves, them!"

The other one nodded.

"Bad thieves! bad thieves!" he said.

Chap now asked the Indians where they supposed the two fellows would take the boat.

"Go up river back here," said the Indian who did the most talking. "Think you won't find 'em and go home. Then they shoot 'gators and have fun."

"But why should they take our boat?" asked Chap. "They have one of their own."

"P'raps she leak. Yours good boat," said the other. "But some men bad, nobody knows why."

To this piece of philosophy the other nodded assent, and then, for a few minutes, the two talked together in their own language.

These men were Seminole Indians, belonging to

the remnant of the powerful tribe which once waged war against the United States and Florida. But the Seminoles who may now occasionally be met in the lower part of the State are generally quiet and peaceable, and glad enough to sell some venison or other game to the sportsmen or tourists they may meet in the forests or on the rivers in the unsettled portions of the State.

When the two Indians had finished their conversation, the talker made a proposition to Chap. He told him that he and his companion, with two others, who were now probably a mile or two away, had come into this part of the country on a hunting expedition; but that, if he would pay them for their trouble, they would go after these fellows and capture the boat.

"River bends 'round here," said the talker, waving his hand behind him, "and they got to sail that way. 'Fraid to keep on big river. You get boat, go after 'em. We go straight through woods, and ketch 'em when they go camp at night. Then bring boat back to you."

Chap stood and considered the matter, and a brilliant plan soon entered his head. If he went back to confer with his companions, a great deal of time would be lost, and there might be diversities of opinion as to what should be done. He felt that the proper thing to do was to follow the Indian's advice, and go a short way through the woods and intercept the fellows when they camped.

They were certain to come on shore to cook their evening meal, and these Indians seemed to know the very spot where they would be likely to land.

"Now," thought Chap, "I've a great mind to put myself at the head of these Indians and recapture The Rolling Stone. Instead of going and telling the other fellows that I've lost the boat, I'll bring it back to them. They're bound to wait for me, and they can find quarters in that house that Adam went to."

Chap thereupon told the Indians that if they and their companions would assist him in recapturing the boat, he would see that they were paid for their time and trouble. He also made them understand that he would lead the expedition, provided that they would show him the way.

To all this the Indians assented, exhibiting a willingness to leave the amount of their remuneration entirely to Chap's generosity, and while one of them started off to find his absent companions, the other set about preparing for Chap a portion of the food that was cooking on the fire, for our friend declared himself nearly famished.

"Isn't this a high old change in things?" said Chap to himself, as he sat watching the Indian stirring the unknown mess in the blackened vessel he had taken from the fire. "Just a little while ago I was hanging about home, expecting to hear that school would begin next day, and here I am, in the wilds of Florida, and about to lead a band of redmen through the trackless forest."

*   *   *   *   *   *   *

Phil and Phœnix wandered for a good distance along the woodland path. Except the birds which they saw flying about above the forest when they occasionally came to an open place in the green roof over them, they found nothing to shoot at.

They had fired a few shots at these, without effect, much to Phil's disappointment, for he wished to take home some trophies of this trip, even if they were nothing but wings and tails of strange birds, when they met Adam returning with two small cans of milk.

The good sailor was in a great hurry to get back to his little bears, and he told the boys that they must come with him, for they would start off now as soon as they could, for he had noticed, when he he was up at the house, that the wind had got round a little to the east, and that they, therefore, would be able to make pretty good headway.

But when the three arrived at the river-side, and found no boat and no Chap and no bears, their astonishment was so great that they could scarcely find words to express it.

"Has that boy gone off with the boat?" at last exclaimed Adam.

"I can scarcely believe it," said Phil, "and yet there's no knowing what Chap would do if an idea suddenly came into his head."

"But Chap can't sail a boat," said Phœnix, "and he would never think of going out in a wind like this. Perhaps the boat got loose accidentally."

"I don't think that happened," said Adam, who was scanning the river with his experienced eye, "for if she's got off, she'd 'a' blown down the river, and I can't see a sign of her. Of course there's no way of her gettin' up-stream ag'in such a wind as this."

As he spoke, Adam turned and looked up-stream, and then he caught sight of the dirty little boat which had been run ashore by the two untidy young men, and with a sudden "Hello!" he ran toward it, followed closely by the boys.

When he reached the boat, the sailor looked at it and in it and around it, but he said not a word.

"Whose boat can this be?" cried Phil. "It couldn't have been here when we came."

"Why, no!" exclaimed Phœnix. "We should certainly have seen it either last night or this morning."

"No," said Adam. "This boat hasn't been here very long, and whoever came in it has gone off in our boat. It's my belief they didn't intend to come back to this little tub, for they've taken everything out of her. They've either coaxed your pardner to go with them, or they've carried him off."

Adam, who knew what desperate characters are occasionally found in this part of the State, where officers of the law seldom make their appearance, and where the few settlers and travellers are obliged to depend in a great measure upon themselves for the preservation of their lives and property, thought for a moment that if Chap had offered opposition to the persons who had taken the boat, there was a probability that he now lay at the bottom of the river. But he said nothing of this to the boys, and he tried to dismiss from his own mind the idea that anything so dreadful had happened.

The people who lived and travelled on the Indian River were generally of a peaceful disposition, although lawless characters were sometimes to be met with, and he tried to believe that this was nothing but some wild freak, perhaps encouraged by the conduct of Chap.

"I tell you what it is!" cried Adam. "Our boat's gone up that small river we passed a mile or two below here. I don't believe she's had time to get out of sight on the main stream. I haven't been away more'n an hour altogether, and there wasn't any boat in sight when I left. What we've got to do is to take this boat and go after her."

"All right," said the boys; and with a will the dirty little craft was pushed off, and the three scrambled in.

CHAPTER XII.

CHAP LEADS THE INDIANS.

It was not long before the Indian who had gone after his two hunting companions returned with them to the place where Chap and the Indian, whom we will call "The Talker," were eating their mid-day meal.

The new-comers were duly introduced to Chap, and expressed their willingness to take part in the expedition. Each of these men carried a rifle, and the smaller and more quiet of the two Indians whom Chap had first met was the only member of the party besides our friend who was not armed.

Chap would have been very glad while leading this expedition to carry a weapon of some kind; but as there was no weapon for him, he resolved to cut a club as soon as he found a suitable limb or sapling.

If he could get a whack at the two fellows who

pushed him out of the boat, he felt that it would do him a great deal of good.

The newly-arrived Indians having made a hasty meal, there was no time lost in starting. Chap placed himself at the head of the party, but he had not gone far before he felt obliged to relinquish that position.

The path along which he had come, and which stretched out westwardly through the forest, was a path worn by persons walking from a landing-place on the tributary river to the spot on the main stream where our friends had made their camp of the night before, which was also a frequently used landing-place.

But the woods now before our party were closely overgrown, and it required eyes better accustomed to the business than those of Chap's to readily find the path.

This passage through the woods was, when the size of the bend of the tributary river was considered, a short cut between the landing-places on the two streams; but it was, for all that, a long walk, and it was late in the afternoon when The Talker announced to Chap that they were approaching the bank of the other river.

"How do we know that we are going to strike the river at the right place to meet the rascals?" asked Chap. "They may land on the opposite bank, and then we can't get at them."

"Only one landin'-place 'long here," said the Indian; "but just where we are goin' to go. Ketch 'em there. You see. Just wait."

The Indians now called a halt, and after a few words among themselves, The Talker informed Chap that they had determined to remain where they were until after nightfall, because, if the men on the boat caught sight of any of them, they would suspect something, and would not land at all.

"Sit down; rest," said The Talker. "I'll go see if boat has come along yit."

"I thought it wouldn't do for you to show yourself," said Chap, sitting down on a fallen tree-trunk, while the three Indians sat upon the ground.

"Ain't goin' to look; goin' to ask," said The Talker, as he disappeared into a by-path, which Chap had not noticed before.

In about half an hour The Talker returned, and, much to Chap's surprise, he was accompanied by a young white girl, carrying a pail.

"This is Mary Brown," said The Talker.

The three Indians then arose, and shook hands with Mary Brown, with whom they seemed to be very well acquainted.

The young girl offered Chap her hand, and said, as she put down her pail,—

"I've brought you some supper; I'd had you come up to the house, but he tells me," pointing to The Talker, "that you don't want to be seen."

"Do you live in these woods?" asked Chap, in amazement.

"Yes," said Mary Brown, "we live about half a mile back thar. 'Tain't on the river, but it's on high ground, with a clearin' 'round it, so that people can be seen pretty plain from the water. He asked me if I'd seed a boat come up to-day, but I'm jist certain none has come up yit, for I'd been sure to see it. I've been watchin' out for father. He's gone up Indian River. I don't 'spect him back to-day, but I might as well watch."

The girl took a piece of corn-bread from her pail, and gave it to Chap, and offered him the first choice of a plate of cold fried bacon. Chap was obliged to take this food in his fingers, but he was glad enough to get it, and said nothing about the absence of plates, knives, and forks.

"I'll bring you down some coffee after a while," said Mary Brown, "but I hadn't made any fire when that Indian came up to the house."

She gave the rest of the corn-bread and bacon to the Indians, and then came and sat down by Chap.

"He tells me," said she, "that some fellows have stole your boat, and that you're goin' to try to take it away from 'em again."

"That is what we started out to do," said Chap,

"but I'm very much afraid this plan won't work. We are not even sure that the men who stole the boat came up this river, for I did not stay to see which way they went; and if they did come up this way, why should they land at the particular place where these Indians expect to find them, and to which there is a track right through the woods from the place where they stole the boat?"

"You let these Indians alone," said the girl, "for knowin' jist what people are goin' to do, 'specially fellers that are huntin' and fishin'. I don't reckon them boat thieves ever heard thar was a good campin'-place up here, but they can't help findin' it out, for all the way up from the mouth of the river there's nothin' but reeds and swamps and 'gators; and when they git to the bit of hard, white sand down thar, which they can see ever so fur away, they'll be sure to come to it. Everybody does who goes along this river, —that is, if they come up this fur. Of course, they may have turned 'round and gone back long ago, but you've got to take your chances of that. As for this track through the woods, I don't suppose they know anything about it, and if they did, they wouldn't 'spect you to find it. And now I must go up to the house, and look out for the boat. You and the Indians had better keep shady till I tell you whether it's comin' or not."

Mary Brown belonged to the class of people

which in Florida are called "crackers." These are poor whites, generally found in the half-settled portions of the State, who make a scanty living by fishing, hunting, and cultivating small patches of ground. They are usually uneducated. As a rule, they are an orderly people, and many of them are by nature intelligent and bright.

Mary Brown had been thrown a good deal on her own resources, and she had learned to take a very common-sense view of the things that came under her observation. She wore a large sun-bonnet, and no shoes or stockings, and seemed afraid of nothing in the shape of man or beast which she might meet in the wild forest that surrounded her solitary home, where at present she was left with her mother and an old negro man, who acted as general helper about the place.

When she had gone, the Indians sat talking among themselves, while Chap folded his arms and stood leaning against a tree.

"I don't half like the way things are going," he said to himself. "It don't seem to me that I'm exactly commanding this party, although I regularly hired them, and took them into my service. They're doing everything just as they please, and I shouldn't wonder if the whole thing should turn out a fizzle. But if we get a chance to do anything, I'll soon let them know that I'm captain."

About fifteen minutes after this, Mary Brown came hurrying to them. She carried a tin-cup of hot coffee, sweetened, but with no milk in it, which she gave to Chap.

"There's a boat comin' up the river," she said, "and of course it's your'n. Now you fellers lie low, and she's bound to land on the beach down thar. I'll go up on the high ground and keep a lookout," and away she ran.

It was growing dark in the woods, but in the cleared space around the Brown's cabin it was light enough for the girl to see the boat come up the river, and steer directly for the sandy beach.

When she returned and told the waiting party that the boat was about to make a landing, Chap, who had been much excited by the news that there was a sail in sight, seized the club he had cut in the woods, and addressed the Indians:

"We must get along now to that landing-place, and the minute the boat touches the shore, we must make a rush at her and capture her."

"No, no," said The Talker; "that won't do. If they hear us while they're in boat, they push off, up sail, and we never see 'em ag'in. Wait till they come ashore, then we fix 'em. No hurry."

Chap was obliged to acknowledge that this was good advice, but he contented himself with the de-

termination that when the decisive moment came
he would not let the Indians do all the fighting.

"We will move quietly down toward the river,"
he said, "and then, when we are sure the boat is
tied up, and they are on shore, we'll make a rush
for them."

"All right," said The Talker.

And slowly and cautiously the party, followed
at a little distance by Mary Brown, made its way
in the direction of the river.

CHAPTER XIII.

ADAM LEADS HIS PARTY.

ADAM and the two boys had not sailed very far
in the dirty little boat, when they found out why
the persons who had been using her had left her
and taken The Rolling Stone in her place.

This little boat, on the stern of which was
painted the name " Maggie," was very leaky, and
required continual bailing. Her sailing tackle was
out of order, and she was a very undesirable boat.
But Phœnix and Phil bailed away bravely with a
couple of tin cans which they found on board, and
Adam, having steered into the mouth of the smaller
river, put the boat before the wind and sailed along
at a good rate.

The stream they were now in twisted and wound
a good deal, and they could not see very far ahead,
but every moment they hoped to come in sight of
The Rolling Stone.

"I cannot imagine," said Phil, "why Chap should have gone off in that boat. If it was taken away from him, or borrowed, I should have supposed he would stay behind to tell us what had become of her."

"If it was took by unfair means," said Adam, "he'd be very likely to think he ought to stick by her to the last, and if they took her they'd have to take him. P'raps they were only goin' a little way up this river, and he's undertook to bring her back."

"If he does, he'll upset her," said Phœnix.

"If that's so," said Adam, "we'll come across her bottom up, and the young chap sittin' on her keel."

"And all our things in the river," said Phil.

"That'll be about it," quietly replied Adam, hoping from the bottom of his heart that nothing worse than this had happened.

About four o'clock, as they rounded a bend in the river, Phil, who was standing by the mast, gave a shout.

"A sail ahead!" he cried.

And, sure enough, about a mile ahead a boat was plainly to be seen.

"That's her!" cried Adam. "Now, boys, load up that gun with buckshot, six in each barrel, and we'll keep after her as long as she's above water."

"The Rolling Stone is a great deal faster than this old thing," said Phœnix, "and I'm afraid we'll never catch up with her."

"We've gained on her now," said Adam, "for she must have been a good deal ahead of us when we started. There isn't much wind up here, with these high trees on each side, and that boat needs a good breeze to make her do her best. If the wind goes down altogether toward sunset, and we have to pole, I'd rather have this boat than that."

Adam now gave his utmost attention to making the best of the breeze, and as he was a better sailor than the men in The Rolling Stone, and as the Maggie could make a fair headway with less wind than the larger boat, she gradually gained upon the latter.

"Look here," said Phil, who, while Phœnix was still bailing away, had been gazing earnestly ahead, "there are only two men on board that boat, and I'm certain that neither of them is Chap."

Phœnix started as he heard these words, and involuntarily looked up at Adam. The sailor said not a word, but his face seemed to have grown hard and dark, and his hand fastened itself upon the tiller with a nervous grip, as if he wished to animate the vessel with his own fierce anxiety to hasten on.

The young men in the other boat evidently knew

that they were pursued, and were doing all that they could to get away.

If there had been a fair wind, The Rolling Stone would have left the other boat far behind; but it soon happened that the Maggie had greatly the advantage.

A portion of the river was now reached where, although the stream was very wide, the water was not over five feet deep, and the bottom, which seemed to be made up entirely of oyster-beds, could plainly be seen.

One of the men on The Rolling Stone was already using a pole to assist the progress of the boat; but when Adam called Phil to the tiller and seized the pole which lay on the deck of the Maggie, it soon became evident that a small boat was much better than a larger one, when each was pushed through the water by means of a pole.

Adam was a strong man and accustomed to hard work, and his vigorous efforts made the Maggie glide so fast through the water that she rapidly gained upon the foremost boat.

As the two were about a dozen yards apart Adam told Phœnix to stand ready to lay hold of the other boat when they should touch.

Phil held the gun, but Adam cautioned him not to be too quick in using it.

When the boats were quite near each other, the

young man who had been poling The Rolling
Stone dropped his pole, and picking up a gun,
raised it to his shoulder. But this did not frighten
the valiant Adam.

"Put down that gun!" he roared, as the two
boats touched.

The young man who had been steering now
rose to his feet. His gun was probably not loaded,
for he did not attempt to pick it up, although it
lay near him.

The two fellows looked sullenly at the party in
the other boat, but they must have felt that it
would be of no use to offer battle.

Adam had picked up a hatchet; Phil had a
double-barrelled gun, and a glance at the strong
figure of Phœnix, who stood with his sleeves rolled
up and his shirt thrown open, was enough to make
any one feel that a tussle with such a fellow was
not a thing to be desired.

Their opponents were three to their two, and
looked like fellows determined to win. It would
not pay to fight, and the untidy young man with
the gun lowered his weapon.

Instantly Adam sprang on board The Rolling
Stone.

"Where's the boy who was on this boat?" he
cried.

"He went ashore when we traded," was the
answer. "Didn't he tell you so?"

"We haven't seen him," said Adam. "Now, if you fellers lie to me, I'll split your heads open with this hatchet. I'll have no foolin'. Where is he?"

The young men looked at each other. They were evidently surprised that the boy from whom they had taken The Rolling Stone had not been seen by his companions. They supposed, of course, that he had told them all about the affair.

"I tell you," said one of them, "we're not foolin'. He went right ashore after we had traded boats."

"Traded boats!" cried Phil, who had laid down his gun. "What do you mean by that?"

"Why, your pardner said you folks only wanted a boat to get up the river, and as this one is to be took back to Brewer, we traded."

"I don't believe a word of it!" cried Phil and Phœnix, almost in a breath.

"It's a lie on the face of it," said Adam, stepping up to the last speaker and lifting his hatchet. "Now, if you scoundrels don't want to be brained right here, you'd better speak out and tell the truth. You stole the boat, and we know it."

"I didn't say the young man was altogether willin' to trade, but we did trade. Didn't we leave our boat? and haven't you got it? We was a-goin' to leave all your things for you, but your pardner, as soon as he went ashore, began a-hollerin' for you all, and we thought you'd be firin' at us the next minute, and so we had to put off."

"You meant to steal this boat and everything in it," said Adam, "and you made that young man go ashore."

"We told him he'd better," said the other.

"Yes," added his companion; "but he got mad, and the minute he set foot on the sand, he ran into the woods a-hollerin' for you all."

Phœnix had said little during this time, but his feelings were rapidly reaching the boiling-point. At this moment he sprang on board The Rolling Stone, and, seizing one of the young men by the collar, he shouted,—

"If I hear any more of that talk, you're going overboard. Where is the boy that was on this boat?"

The young man thus suddenly attacked raised his arm to defend himself, but Adam pushed between the two.

"Don't fight yet," he said to Phœnix. "We'll see directly what's to be done to 'em."

This remark frightened the two rascals more than anything that had been yet said or done. It seemed to indicate a determination to inflict some sort of punishment upon them, and if these three excited persons believed that their companion had been made away with, there was nothing to prevent them from taking summary vengeance upon their captives, and throwing their bodies to the alligators. On these lonely waters they could expect no help.

"I tell you," said one of the young men, very earnestly, "it's all truth that we've been sayin'. The whole thing was a lark, and we wouldn't 'a' done it if we hadn't been drinkin'. We was a-sayin' just before we seed you comin' after us that we was sorry we took your boat, and if there was a good wind to-morrer, we'd overhaul you and give her back to you. We haven't hurt none of your things, and we've fed your little bears with the milk we brought along for ourselves."

"Yes," said Adam, grimly; "that's because you wanted to raise 'em and sell 'em."

"No," said the other. "We was a-goin' to give 'em back to you."

No answer was made to this palpable falsehood, and every one seemed to hesitate before making the next move. Then Adam spoke up.

"We've got to talk this thing over," said he to Phil and Phœnix. Then, turning to the untidy young men, he told them to get into their own boat, and pull her out of ear-shot. "And mind you don't try to get away," he added, as the fellows scrambled into the Maggie; "for if you do I'll put a dozen buckshot into you before you know it."

One of the young men poled his boat away until

Adam called to him to stop, and then our three friends sat down to talk the matter over. There was a gentle current in the stream, and the two boats floated slowly along without diminishing the distance between them.

"What do you both think about it?" asked Phil, nervously.

"I think they are a pair of scoundrels," said Phœnix, "and they ought to be knocked on the head."

"We can't do that," said Adam, "though I'd shoot 'em quick enough if it had to be done to save any of us; but I feel pretty sure that Chap's all right, though the story of these fellers is an out-and-out lie. They just took the boat from him, and made off with it, and that's all there is about it."

"One part of their story seemed probable," said Phil, "and that was that Chap got mad and bolted into the woods after us. He isn't the fellow to stand still and see his property taken off without making a fuss."

"No, indeed!" added Phœnix, earnestly.

"If their story is true," said Adam, "and Chap ran into the woods after us, he must have taken the wrong track, or we would have seen him. There is a path which leads to the left not very far from the beach."

"Yes," said Phil, "Phœnix and I noticed that,

and debated a little which way we should go, and finally concluded to keep to the right."

"Yes," said Adam, "that's what he must 'a' done, and that's the way we missed him. I don't believe them fellers did anything to him. There couldn't 'a' been any need of it, for I 'spect they sneaked off with the boat while he was on shore."

"And what are we going to do about it?" said Phœnix. "Let them off scot free while we go back after Chap?"

"Well," said Adam, "we can't very well kill the rascals, and it wouldn't pay to hold on to 'em. The best thing we can do is to get rid of 'em as soon as we can."

"And then go back after Chap," suggested Phœnix.

"I don't know about that," said Adam, a little absently.

He was looking at Phil, and noticed that the boy was very pale and silent, and that he sat doubled up as if he felt weak and tired.

Not one of the party had eaten anything since breakfast. They had been so excited and so eager to overtake the stolen boat, and find out what had become of Chap, that the thought of food had not entered their minds. Phœnix and Adam were both very robust, and the omission of a single meal had not affected them; but Phil, although he was a healthy fellow, was not so hardy and so capable of sustaining privations as his companions, and Adam could see that he was really faint for want of food.

"I don't think we'll make anything by startin' back now," he said. "It'll be dark in an hour or two, and then we couldn't sail on this crooked river, and we'd have to anchor and wait for mornin'. We couldn't land and make a fire and have anything hot and comfortable for supper, for there isn't a spot we've passed where we could go ashore. But I see a bit of sandy beach way up ahead there, and there we can land and boil some coffee, and have a good meal, and I'm sure we all need it."

"But what about poor Chap all this time?" asked Phil, looking up.

"Oh, I haven't forgot Chap!" said Adam; "and I don't think we need be troubled about him. When he got down to the beach he'd know that we'd gone off in the boat that was left there, and that we'd come back ag'in. He'd be sure to go and look for the house when he felt hungry, and as he wouldn't take the wrong track the second time, he'd find it easy enough. There's no gittin' really lost in them woods, for there's no gittin' out of the beaten tracks, and they always lead somewhere. So it stands to reason he's better off than we are, as far as comfort goes. And we can't get to him till to-morrer, no matter when we start. So

12*

I say we'll go up there to that beach and have our supper. I don't want either one of you sick on my hands, for that would be the worst thing that could happen."

"But what about those two fellows?" asked Phœnix.

"We'd better let them get out of sight just as fast as they can," said Adam. "If they can't find any place to camp it'll serve 'em right. It's not our business to make 'em comfortable, and they can't stay where we are. So I say let's put their things on their old boat and tell them to make themselves scarce."

The boys both agreed that in regard to Chap and the two untidy young men there did not seem to be anything to do but to follow Adam's advice. The Maggie was, therefore, hailed and ordered to come alongside.

"Now, look here," said Adam to the two men; "you've got to get out of this just as fast as you can, for we've agreed that we can't keep our hands off o' you more'n half an hour longer. We'll give you back your dirty things, for we don't want none of your property. But I'm not goin' to give you back your guns, for one of 'em is a rifle, an' you're just the fellers to take a crack at us after you got out of range of our shot-gun. I'll leave the guns for you at Titusville, at the hotel. You can't have 'em while we're on the river."

The young men demurred very much at being deprived of their firearms, but Adam's determination was not moved, and they were obliged to go away and leave their guns on The Rolling Stone.

The wind served them better going down the stream than coming up, and so, with pole and sail, and the assistance of the current, they soon put a good distance between themselves and the other boat, feeling in their hearts that if they did not make haste enough, a ball from their own rifle might overtake them. They were so cowardly themselves that they expected every one else to be so.

CHAPTER XIV.

CHAP'S AMBASSADOR.

THE stretch of white sand, of which Adam had spoken, was so far away that neither of the boys had noticed it; but the practised eyes of the sailor had singled it out as a place where a landing could be made, and toward it The Rolling Stone was now steered, Phœnix taking the tiller, and Adam using the pole whenever he could.

Phil was ordered to refresh himself with some crackers and cold meat, as it would be some time before they could have their coffee.

"I'm not going to eat anything," said Phœnix, "till we have cooked a regular supper; but I tell you it's jolly to think of getting something good and hot when we land."

"That's so," said Adam.

And Phil assented heartily. But not one of them imagined how hot a thing was waiting for them.

140

The Rolling Stone thus moving slowly up the
river, gradually came into sight of the keen-eyed
maiden, who surveyed the water from the high
ground in the vicinity of the Browns' cabin, and,
as we have seen, she informed Chap and his
companions of its approach.

When the boat at last touched the shore, it was
still light by the river, and Chap and the Indians
were well concealed in the dusky recesses of the
forest, not far from the water; and over the underbrush and between the trees Chap could catch
sight of the little red pennant, made from an old
handkerchief which he himself had hoisted to the
topmast of The Rolling Stone.

The sight made him furious to rush down and
recapture his boat; but the others restrained him.
It was not time yet. The fellows must have no
chance to push off and get away.

"Look here," said Mary Brown, who had closely
followed Chap's party, "I wish there wasn't goin'
to be a fight. I'd hate to see people killed so near
our house. I've been thinkin' of a good thing to
do, and I'll tell you what it is. I'll go down and
talk to them fellers. They won't be scared off
when they see a girl comin', and then I'll just tell
'em the whole thing. I'll tell 'em there are five
of you here, and you're bound to have the boat
back, and they might as well give it up first as last,
and not have nobody shot."

" And as soon as you began to talk that way,"
said Chap, " they'd all jump aboard and push
off."

" No, they wouldn't," said the girl; " for I
wouldn't talk to 'em if they wasn't all ashore, and
the minute any of 'em started to go aboard, I'd
give a scream, and then you all could come peltin'
down."

" And what would we do with them," asked
Chap, a little contemptuously, " if they agreed to
all that?   Let them walk off, scot-free?"

" There ain't no use a-doin' anythin' to 'em,"
said Mary Brown, " when you've got your boat.
That's all you want."

The Indians, who understood all that Mary
Brown said, and had listened to her with great
attention, now expressed themselves as well satisfied with the plan she proposed.   If the men
would give up the boat without fighting, what
was the good of fighting?   But this did not satisfy
Chap.

" I want the rascals punished," he said.

" Humph!" said The Talker.   " S'pose you first
one shot.   Won't do you no good then to lick
'em."

" They won't believe you," said Chap to Mary,
" when you tell them there are five of us.   They'll
think it a trick."

" That's their lookout," said the girl.   " If they

don't believe me, you can pitch into 'em; but you oughter try first to do without fightin'."

Finding that his companions were very unwilling to resort to violence, if the boat could be regained peacefully, Chap was obliged to submit, and Mary Brown started off to treat for a surrender of The Rolling Stone.

"Mind," she said, as she left, "if they cut up, or try to get back into their boat, I'll scream, and then you all come."

"Oh, we'll come quick enough!" said Chap, clutching his club. "You needn't be afraid of that."

When Mary Brown went out on the river-beach, she saw only Adam and Phil, for Phœnix had gone up the shore to look for dry sticks for the fire. She walked up to our two friends, who were quite surprised to see her, not knowing that there was any habitation in the neighborhood, and after wishing them "good-evening," she related to them the purpose of her mission.

While she was speaking, Phœnix came up, and his appearance made her quite uneasy. She had supposed there were only two persons in the boat, but if there were three, it would make the fight a great deal worse, if there should be one, and she therefore urged, with increased earnestness, that they should give up the boat peaceably, before they were set upon by the determined men in the woods.

"Give us a moment to think this over," said Adam, when she had finished.

And the girl retired to a short distance, while our friends drew close together in anxious consultation.

"Those two rascals," said Adam, "must have waded ashore somewhere, and come across these Indians. And now they're a-goin' to try to take the boat from us. They've had time enough to get around here, for we came up very slow."

"Perhaps it's all a made-up story," said Phœnix.

"That couldn't be," said Phil, "for how would that girl know that we had taken the boat from anybody?"

"Whether her story is true or not," said Adam, "we're not goin' to give up the boat, are we?"

"No, indeed!" answered both of the boys.

"I'm glad we took the guns from them fellers," said Adam, "for now we've each got one. Let's jump aboard and get the shootin'-irons. That's the first thing to do."

The three now moved toward the boat, which had been drawn up in shallow water.

"Don't go aboard yit!" exclaimed Mary, quickly stepping toward them; but, as no attention was paid to her words, she gave a loud scream, and ran into the woods.

CHAPTER XV.

THE FORCES MEET.

It so happened that the three guns on The Rolling Stone were all loaded, and as they sprang on board, Adam, Phil, and Phœnix each snatched up one of them.

"Cover yourselves and be ready!" cried Adam.

And, at these words, Phil bounced into the little cabin and put his gun out the landward window; Phœnix stepped on the little strip of deck on the other side of the cabin, and crouching behind it, rested his gun upon the roof, while Adam threw himself flat down on the bottom of the boat and pointed his gun over the side.

"Cock your guns," cried Adam, "but don't fire till I give the word. I hear 'em comin'."

The moment that Mary Brown's scream was heard, Chap sprang toward the river, followed by the four Indians.

"Hold back!" cried The Talker. "You take care! You be shot!"

But Chap paid no attention to this warning. His only idea was to rush upon the two marauders and whang them over the head with his club.

It was now almost dark in the woods, but on the water and the river beach objects could be easily seen.

The Talker thrust his gun into the hands of the unarmed Indian, and making a dash at Chap, he seized him around the waist just as he was about to rush out into the open.

"That no way to fight," he cried. "You be shot."

Encircling the boy with his strong arms, he held him back. Then, speaking to one of the other Indians, he told him to peep out and see how matters stood.

The Indian quickly reported that the men were in the boat, and had their guns levelled at the shore.

"Bad rascals," said The Talker. "Goin' to try kill somebody and keep boat. You hold him," continued The Talker, giving Chap into the custody of one of the other Indians, "and we go fix 'em."

Taking his gun again, The Talker and two of his companions stepped to the edge of the woods, where each immediately slipped behind a tree.

"Let me go!" cried Chap, while struggling with the Indian who was holding him. "I'm captain of this party, and you've no right to keep me back."

To this appeal the Indian made no answer, but held on vigorously to the wrathful boy.

"There went three of 'em behind them trees," said Adam. "I know they're Indians by the way they move, and they've got guns. The white fellers are keepin' back."

"That's because we've got their guns," cried Phil, from the cabin.

"They'd do it anyhow," said Adam,—"the cowards! These Indians 'll be bad customers and hard to hit. Don't fire if they don't come out, and keep yourselves as well covered as you kin."

The Talker now shouted from behind his tree,—

"Come ashore! Give up boat! We let you off!"

The impudence of this demand exasperated the boys, and Phil, now strengthened by excitement and his meal of cold meat and crackers, sent back a shout of defiance. But Adam exclaimed,—

"Keep quiet! 'Tain't no use to waste breath on 'em. Let's see what they'll do next."

Again The Talker shouted that if they didn't get out of that boat, and give it up, he and his men would come down and take it.

"All right!" said Adam to the boys. "As long as they stick behind them trees, we couldn't hit 'em, even if 'twas daylight, but if they rush down on us we can fire at 'em as quick as we please, and the law'll stand by us, for we've got a right to fight for our property when there's nobody to do it for us. So let 'em come, if they want to."

But the Indians behind the trees did not seem inclined to do anything in a hurry.

They might have fired at the people on the boat, and, perhaps, have hit them, for they were not perfectly protected, nor were their defences bullet-proof; but although these Indians, in this wild country, were, in a measure, outside the pale of the law, they knew that to deliberately shoot human beings, who had so far offered them no violence, would be very much like a murder.

They had not expected to meet a party so well armed, and ready to protect themselves, for they had expected to rush in between the marauders and their stolen boat, and, by their superiority and numbers, to effect a speedy victory.

They spoke to each other from tree to tree, and it is possible that they contemplated waiting until night had really set in, when, under cover of the darkness, they could slip down and capture the boat without so much danger of being shot.

But Chap was out of all patience with this ridiculous delay.

"What's the good of standing there and hollerin'," he said, "instead of going down and doing something? The first thing you know those fellows will push the boat off, and get away with her."

"Don't be 'fraid," said the Indian who still held him. "We keep eye on 'em. No get 'way."

But Chap's active mind and body could not be content with talk like this. With a sudden and powerful wrench he broke away from the Indian who was holding him, and, brandishing his club, he rushed out upon the beach.

He would show them what to do. If he dashed down upon the boat, the Indians were bound to follow, and the rascals would be overpowered in a second.

The moment he appeared upon the beach, three guns were levelled at him, and three nervous fingers trembled upon the triggers.

Suddenly Phil, who happened to have the rifle, dropped the muzzle of his piece, and, raising his head, looked boldly out of the cabin window. At the same instant Phœnix's head popped up from behind the cabin, and Adam sprang to his feet.

Then from all three came the single word,—

"Chap!"

On hearing his name pronounced by these familiar voices, Chap stopped suddenly and lowered his club. Then, without reflecting that they were exposing themselves to the aim of the ruthless red men, Phil, Adam, and Phœnix sprang from the boat, the two boys in their excitement leaving their guns on board, and rushing toward their stupefied companion.

The Indians, seeing their ally thus set upon, were inclined to fire, but, apart from the probability of their hitting Chap, there was something so peculiar in his attitude, and in the actions of those who had rushed upon him, that they forbore.

Running down to the group on the beach, they reached it in time to see Chap dancing about, and apparently shaking hands with all three of his friends at once, while myriads of questions, without any answers to balance them, flew wildly about in every direction.

The Indians, amazed at this strange scene, stood silently looking on, while Mary Brown, who had been hidden somewhere in the woods, came down and listened with open mouth and eyes.

It was at least five minutes before Chap or his friends could get fairly started in an explanation of what had happened. At last, through the rattling noise of question, answer, and exclamation, the stories were straightened out, and everybody, even the Indians, began to understand what had really happened, and how it had come to pass.

"Well," cried Phil, "you ought to be thankful, Chap, for your legs."

"Legs?" said Chap.

"Yes," answered Phil, laughing. "The moment I got a good sight of them, I remembered that besides Chap Webster, there wasn't another fellow of fifteen with a thirty-year old pair of legs."

"I saw 'twas a boy, too," said Adam, "and he skipped down in a way that seemed to me mighty nat'ral to somebody."

"They are a good pair of legs," said Chap, looking down at his long extremities, "and they often come in handy."

"Now then," cried Adam, "we'll build a fire and have our supper as soon as we can, and we'll do the rest of our talkin' while we are eatin'."

It was almost too dark now to find firewood, but everybody helped to look for it.

One of the Indians went to a spring near by for water. Very soon a bright fire was blazing upon the beach, a potful of coffee was bubbling on the coals, while a pan of bacon sizzled near by.

There was enough for all, and everybody was invited to the repast, the cups, saucers, and plates from The Rolling Stone being made to do as much duty as possible.

Mary Brown declined to stay to supper.

"Mother 'll be a-wonderin' what's become of

me," she said, "and she can't send old Job down to see, cos she don't want to be left by herself. I'm mighty glad you didn't have a fight, but I was so afeared you was goin' to be shot," she said, addressing Chap, "that I jist clapped my sun-bonnet down over my eyes, and I didn't know nothin' what happened till I looked up and see you all dancin' round and shakin' hands. If any of you want anything to help camp, you can come up to the house and see if you can git it."

And then with a nod which seemed to be made to the party in general, the girl ran home.

After half an hour of talk, our friends stowed themselves away in the cabin of The Rolling Stone, and the Indians made themselves as comfortable as possible on the sand at the edge of the woods.

The sand was dry, the air was mild, and these hardy red men were very glad to have a bed so smooth and soft.

"It is awful funny," said Chap, before he went to sleep, "to think that I was leading a band of Indians through the woods to pounce down on you fellows. And yet, when I come to think of it, I wasn't leading them so very much, either. Seems to me the people down this way don't have the right idea of what a captain ought to be."

"Do you mean us?" said Phil, who shared the narrow bed.

"Well, I don't know," answered Chap. "Your notions do seem to be a little loose ; but I guess I'll get you better disciplined after a while."

"All right," said Phil.

And he went to sleep.

CHAPTER XVI.

MARY BROWN SENDS A MESSAGE.

THE next morning every one was up and stirring long before sunrise. The Indians were well satisfied with a dollar apiece for their services, which had been truly valuable, for they had conducted Chap right into the arms of his friends, although the undertaking had been accompanied by great danger to all concerned, and they took a hasty breakfast and started off to continue their hunting expedition.

While the boys and Adam were still eating their morning meal, Mary Brown came down to the river. She had a clean sun-bonnet and wore shoes and stockings. These seemed to interfere a good deal with her comfort in walking; but it was quite evident that she had dressed herself in her best for this visit, and most people are willing to sacrifice some comfort when they wish to look very well, indeed.

"Mother says she would have come down to see you," said Mary Brown; "but she's got the rheumatism in her knee-bones, and can't walk much. She wanted to see you all, for there ain't many people who come here, and when they do come, they're pretty rough."

"I think we look pretty rough," said Phil, smiling, as he glanced around at the blue shirts and travel-stained garments of his companions.

"Clothes ain't everything," said Mary; "but if thar was a church here, you'd do to go."

"Where *do* you go to church?" asked Chap, as he rose from his breakfast.

"Me?" said Mary Brown, with a smile. "Why, I was never at church in my life."

Chap looked surprised, and although the others were gathering up the breakfast things and preparing to depart, he continued to talk to Mary Brown.

The girl had been very kind to him. Besides this, she interested him. He had never before met with a young person of that kind.

"Have you never been anywhere but just here?" he asked.

"Oh, yes," said she. "I've been up Indian River two or three times to Cooper's store with father, and once I went up to Titusville, but that was a long time ago. I only remember that it was a great big place, with lots of houses and ever so many people. There may have been girls there, but I don't remember seein' any of 'em."

"It must be dreadful to live in these woods always," said Chap.

"There's nothin' dreadful about it," replied Mary Brown. "The b'ars and wild cats and painters won't trouble you if you don't trouble 'em, and the Indians that come along sometimes is just the same as tame white men. But I would kind o' like to see other places. Father's travelled about a good deal, and he's telled me a lot of what he seed. He once went up to Jacksonville, and he's been to Tallahassee, and in some of the places he says there are so many houses that they touch each other. But I always thought he was makin' fun when he told me this. Why, when you had muddy feet, you'd either have to walk right through your house, or else go round the whole town to get to your back door. I can't believe town-people is such fools as that."

Chap laughed.

"I wish you could see a good big city for yourself," said he.

"I'd like to," replied the girl; and then changing the conversation, she asked, "Have you got a sister?"

"Yes," said Chap,—"one."

"What is her name?"

"Helen," answered Chap.

"Can she read?" asked the girl.

"Oh, yes," said Chap.

"And write, too, I s'pose?"

"Yes," was the reply, "she can do all that."

"I'd like something awfully much," said Mary Brown, "and I don't reckon it 'ud be real bothersome to anybody who knows how to write already. I wish, after you git home, you'd ask your sister to write me a small letter. I never got a letter in all my life. I can't read, but father'd read it to me."

"She'll do it," said Chap, warmly. "I know she will. But where shall she direct it? She can't send a letter here."

"Oh, there's a post-office at Cooper's store," said the girl, "and when father goes thar, they tells him if there's a letter thar for him."

Phœnix now called to Chap that they were nearly ready to start.

"Good-by!" said Chap, holding out his hand. "You've been a real trump, and I'll make Helen write you a letter. She'll tell you just how we got home."

Adam and the other boys now came up, and shook hands with Mary Brown. There had been some talk at breakfast of offering to pay her for the provisions she had furnished the night before, but now it had been determined not to do so for

14

fear of offending her. She had evidently offered what she had out of pure good will.

As The Rolling Stone was pushed off, Mary Brown stood upon the beach and watched the departing boat.

"Don't you forget the letter," she called after Chap.

"No, indeed!" shouted Chap, heartily. "You needn't be afraid of that."

"Goin' to write to her?" asked Adam, with a grin.

"No, I'm not," said Chap, his face flushing a little, "but my sister Helen is. It'll be a piece of out-and-out charity. That poor girl never got a letter in her life."

"How are you going to send it?" asked Phœnix. "Per alligator?"

"No," said Chap; "per land-shark; the man who keeps the store up the river."

The girl stood on the beach until the boat was nearly out of sight. She then took off her shoes and stockings, and walked slowly homeward.

"I wish he'd brought his sister with him," she said to herself, as she plodded along toward the lonely house. "If I could 'a' had jist one look at another girl 'twould 'a' been something."

"I hope we'll get to that store of Cooper's early in the afternoon," said Adam, "for if we don't my little bears 'll be out of milk ag'in."

"That will be too bad," said Phil, "for they've got on splendidly so far. No matter what happened to the boat, they've always had their regular meals."

"Yes," said Adam, "them rascals 'spected to make money out of these bears, and they fed 'em up first-rate, but that's the only good thing they did do. They've made us lose pretty nigh two whole days, besides comin' within an inch of havin' a reg'lar battle among ourselves. That was about the last thing I thought could happen."

"I suppose that part of it was my fault," said Chap. "I oughtn't to have tried to get back the boat without letting you know about it."

"It was just as much my fault," said Phil. "If I hadn't gone off, and taken Phœnix, those fellows wouldn't have tried to run off with the boat."

"If it comes to that," remarked Adam, "you might as well say it was my fault; for if I hadn't them little bears, and gone to get milk for 'em, nothin' would 'a' happened. But I say it's nobody's fault. We all did the best we could, and there's the end of it."

When our party reached the main stream, they found a fair wind blowing from the east. This was very favorable for them, and they reached Cooper's store about the middle of the afternoon.

"By the way," said Phil, "it's rather curious that we didn't overtake that dirty little Maggie, with the two boat-thieves aboard."

"I reckon," said Phœnix, "that as soon as she got out of that small river she went down-stream, instead of going up, as we did; but she must have made pretty good time to get out into Indian River before us; for, of course, she couldn't sail at night."

"No," said Adam, "but they started a good deal earlier than we did. They didn't stop to cook breakfast and bid good-by to girls."

"Neither did we," cried Chap, promptly,— "that is, we only waited for breakfast. I didn't keep you waiting a minute."

"That's so," said Adam; "and as to that Maggie, I am pretty sure I saw her when we got out into this river. She was about two miles down the stream on the other side, with her sail down, and most likely anchored."

"What was she doing there?" asked Phœnix.

"My 'pinion is," said Adam, "that she was lyin' there waitin' for us to come out. I think them fellers intend to follow us up to Titusville, keepin' out of our way as much as they kin. You see we've got their guns, and they can't do much till they get 'em."

"I wish they had their old guns," said Phil, "and were sailing down the Indian River. I don't think it's very pleasant to have such fellows sneaking after us."

"I wish they had their guns, too," said Adam, "and if I was only sure they'd sail straight down the river, I'd go in for givin' 'em back to 'em. But I don't trust 'em. They're mean, cowardly scoundrels, and if they could take a crack at us with that rifle afore they went down the river, they'd be quick enough to do it."

"They haven't anything to complain of," said Phil, "for I'm sure we treated them a great deal better than they deserved, or had any right to expect."

"I should say so," cried Chap, vehemently. "If I'd been along, they wouldn't have got off so easily. Just imagine their pushing me slam-bang into the water right off our own boat. It makes me boil over to think of it. If ever I get a chance, I'll pay them up for that."

"I don't suppose you ever will get a chance," said Phœnix; "but if you do, you'd better let them alone. You are rid of them now, and you ought to be glad of it."

"It seems to me, Phœnix," said Chap, "that you are always telling fellows to keep peaceable, and yet, whenever there's a chance to fight, you are the very first one to pitch in."

Phœnix hesitated for a moment. and then he said,—

"Sometimes things are different from what they are at other times."

"All right," said Chap. "Those rascals are out of sight and reach now, and I'll be as peaceable as anybody; but if ever I get within three feet of them, things will be different."

And here the conversation on the subject closed.

"I think you are right, Adam," said Phil. "It wouldn't be safe to let those fellows have their guns till we are off this river. They were very angry when we made them go away without them."

After some further conversation, it was agreed that, although it was very desirable to rid themselves of the companionship of the Maggie and her occupants, it would be wise to keep the guns taken from the boat-thieves until they reached Titusville.

They had, perhaps, no legal right to do this; but they felt that, on general principles of justice, they had a right to protect their lives, and that this was the way to do it.

CHAPTER XVII.

THE CHANNEL-BASS.

The stop at Cooper's store was not a long one. After buying some articles of food that they needed, not forgetting a good supply of condensed milk for the little bears, they set sail again.

As this was a post-office, the boys had inquired for letters. They had no reason to expect any, and they got none; but each of them bought a postal-card and mailed a brief message to his family.

There was a good camping-ground, with spring water, six or seven miles above, and this they reached about nightfall.

The next day they started off early, and as they sailed along with a good wind, they passed a large and comfortable-looking house on the west bank, and saw, now and then, dwellings and clearings, which proved that they would find the country better settled as they sailed northward.

163

They also met a very neatly-appointed yacht, with a good-sized cabin, and among the persons on board were some ladies and children.

"I didn't suppose we'd meet any ladies down in this part of the world," said Phil.

"Oh, yes," said Adam. "When I was in these parts before, ladies who were travelling in the State, and had pluck enough to get to this river, used to come down this fur, but they never went much further South. From here up to Titusville you can gin'rally find houses, about a day's sail apart, where people can stay all night. But some of the boats you can hire up to Titusville are good big ones, with comfortable cabins, and little stoves to cook meals on board, and everything convenient. But I wouldn't want to navigate one of 'em heavy boats, 'cept where the river was deep and wide; and ladies and children haven't no call, anyway, to go much below this. The country's too wild for 'em."

About noon, Adam said,—

"If we had time to fish, we might have good sport just now. This part of the river is a first-rate place to catch channel-bass."

"Let's stop, anyway," cried Chap. "We might fish an hour without hurting anybody. What difference will it make if we get to Boontown an hour earlier or later? And it may be that we'll never get another chance to fish for channel-bass; that is, if this river is the only place where they can be caught."

Phil was entirely of Chap's opinion, and Adam had no objections to fish for a time, if the boys cared for the sport. But Phœnix was not altogether satisfied with the proposed stoppage.

"If we're trying to get home as fast as we can," he said, "I think we oughtn't to stop if we can help it, especially as we've lost so much time anyway."

"But this won't be much time lost," said Phil, "and as I am quartermaster of this party, I think it is my duty to provide you with some fresh food, and we've nothing on hand but salt ham and some of those potted things we got at Cooper's store."

"That sounds as if you intended to catch all the fish," said Chap.

"Of course, if you all want to stop," said Phœnix, "I've nothing more to say."

"Now," said Chap, standing up and raising his right arm as he spoke, "I want to make a remark. It seems to be forgotten that I'm captain of this expedition. But I have not forgotten it, and I order a halt for an hour's fishing."

"After we've all agreed to it," said Phil.

"And as to you, Mr. Treasurer," continued Chap, addressing Phœnix, and paying no attention to Phil's remark, "I wish to say that if you don't stop criticising and opposing your noble commander, I shall depose you from your position."

"All right," said Phœnix, with a grin. "If any other fellow has got capital enough to run the office, I'm willing."

"On second thought," said Chap, "I think we won't request you to resign. As the treasurer of this expedition has to furnish the money, you are the most worthy person for the post. Consider your place secure as long as your cash holds out. Now, Mr. Steersman, shall we anchor?"

"Just jump forward there, cap'n," said Adam, "and when I give the word, let down the mainsail."

It took somewhat longer to make the preparations for fishing than the boys had supposed it would, for Adam had to run the boat ashore on a little island, and wade into the shallow water with a hand-net to catch some small fish for bait.

But at last the boat was put out into deep water, the sails were lowered, and the anchor down, while the three boys, posting themselves in convenient places in the after-part of the boat, threw out their lines as far as they could.

There was quite a strong current at this point, and this helped to carry the lines out to their full length.

Adam did not fish. In the first place he was willing to hold himself ready to direct and assist the boys, and in the second place he had no fishing lines.

"What is a channel-bass?" asked Phil. "I don't think I ever heard of them."

"Well," said Adam, "it's a kind of bass that swims in the channel of this river, and that's pretty much all there is about it."

"Is it a large fish, or a small one?" asked Chap.

Adam was not inclined to give the boys any information on the subject. He wanted them to find out for themselves what a channel-bass was.

"Whatever they are," said Phœnix, after a time, "they seem to be pretty scarce; I haven't had a bite yet."

"Nor I either," said both Chap and Phil.

"They ain't packed in the river like sardines in a box," said Adam, "but I reckon one of 'em will come along after a while."

"I thought I had a bite," said Phœnix, after suddenly giving his line a little jerk, "but I believe my hook has fouled on something at the bottom." Then, after another pull, he exclaimed, "It's loose now, but there's nothing on it. Hook, sinker, and all must have gone!"

And he began disconsolately pulling in his slackened line.

Suddenly the cord, which seemed to be merely floating in the water, straightened out with a jerk, and a yard or two of it ran through Phœnix's fingers, burning like a hot iron.

Then, as the boy nervously grasped the cord with a tighter hold, he was pulled forward with such force that he fell plump upon his knees.

Adam sprang to help Phœnix, but as he did so, the boy rose to his feet.

"Whatever it was," said Phœnix, "it's off again. The line is perfectly slack."

"Haul in! haul in!" cried Adam; "you've got one. Don't let your line be slack, or he'll get off."

Phœnix, now quite excited, rapidly pulled in his line.

When it had become taut again, Adam said,—

"Pull in, but not too hard, or you'll break your line. If he tries to rush off, give him a little line, but if he comes this way, haul in your slack as fast as you can, or he'll get off the hook."

Phœnix worked away bravely, the other boys looking on with excited interest.

He pulled his line in steadily and slowly for a time; then, when the fish seemed determined to run away from him, he let out a few yards; and when it turned and swam toward the boat, he hauled in the slackened line with great rapidity.

In this way he gradually drew his fish nearer

and nearer to the boat, and at last it became tired, and he was able, with occasional stops when the fish gave a short struggle, to pull it slowly in.

Everybody gazed earnestly at the line, and directly they saw, rising from the water, close to the boat, a head as big as a dinner-plate. There was a jerk, as if the fish decidedly objected to poking its nose into the open air, but Adam, who was leaning over the side of the boat, ready for the work of the moment, quickly stretched out his arm and slipped his hand under the fish's gill. Then, with a powerful effort, he rose to his feet, and drew out of the water a channel-bass, over four feet long, and weighing probably forty pounds.

The boys could not find words to express their astonishment and delight when they viewed this prize.

"That's what a channel-bass is!" cried Phil. "If I'd known what whoppers they were, I wouldn't have supposed we could catch one with our lines."

"Your lines are strong," said Adam, "and your hooks pretty good-sized, but if we were comin' out o' purpose for channel-bass, we'd have heavier tackle. But it would be hard work to haul in a feller like this with any line, if you didn't play him right."

After being pulled into the boat, the great bass

did not struggle as long as some of the smaller fish they had caught, and he soon lay quiet and dead.

The boys rolled up their lines, for there were no more bites, and it was agreed that, having found out what a channel-bass was, they ought to be satisfied.

"Is the fish good to eat?" said Phil.

"Tip-top," answered Adam. "We'll cover him up and take him along, and we can have steaks enough for supper to-night and to-morrow's break-fast, and plenty left for the birds besides."

"Well," cried Chap, who had been standing in a reflective mood, "this is the way things always happen. Here is Phœnix, who didn't want to stop and fish, and who grumbled and croaked, and didn't believe there were any fish in the river, even after he got to work; and *he* must catch the channel-bass, while Phil and I, who were in for the thing from the beginning, and full of honest ardor, didn't get a bite. Haul up the sails and pull in the anchor, and let us away! It's no use struggling against blind luck. Virtue and enthusiasm don't count."

This speech was received with a wild laugh, and with four merry hearts and a big fish on board, The Rolling Stone set out again upon her north-ward course.

Adam knew exactly where he intended to

camp that night, and before dark he reached the beach of a little bay upon the eastern shore of the river.

After a hearty supper, of which channel-bass was the principal dish, and a talk by the camp-fire while Adam smoked his evening pipe, our party made everything secure for the night, and were soon asleep in their little cabin.

Chap, as we have said before, was a very early riser, and the next morning he awoke and slipped quietly out of his narrow quarters without awakening any of his companions.

As he gazed around with great delight upon the beautiful morning scene, he saw, scarcely a hundred feet from the spot where they were moored, a dirty little boat anchored near the shore.

"Upon—my—word," said Chap to himself, "if that Maggie hasn't put in here in the night!"

CHAPTER XVIII.

CHAP BOARDS THE MAGGIE.

WHEN Chap Webster stood alone on the deck of The Rolling Stone in the bright, cool air of the early morning and gazed at the dirty little sail-boat, which lay near the shore a short distance above, his feelings were of a very confused nature.

At first he was simply astonished to see the Maggie lying so near them. He had supposed that the fellows who had stolen the boat would be afraid to come near the people they had injured. But, after all, it was no use to be surprised at the impudence of such men. For some reason or other they had stolen in here, either at night or very early in the morning.

The bow of the Maggie was toward Chap, and the little cabin prevented him from seeing anybody who might be in the stern; but very soon

172

it was evident that there were persons on board of her, and that they were awake.

There was a slight noise of people moving about, and directly the heads of the two men were seen above the cabin. Chap instinctively dodged behind the cabin of his own boat, but he kept his eyes fixed on the two fellows, one of whom presently put a water-keg upon his shoulders, and then, with rolled-up trousers and bare feet, both of them waded ashore.

They had anchored their boat in about a foot of water, thinking that if they ran her on the sand, they might not be able to get off in a hurry if occasion required them to do so.

It was now plain enough why they had come in here. They were out of fresh water, and this was the only place for miles where any could be obtained.

As he looked upon the two men who had treated him so badly and who had been the cause of so much trouble and imminent danger to the whole party, Chap began to feel angry. He had believed and steadily asserted that the rascals had been let off entirely too easily, and now his whole soul became filled with a desire to punish them for their misdeeds. If he could meet them, one at a time, he would undertake to give them in turn a good thrashing; but the cowards always kept together, and he did not care to wake up his companions to assist in the desired acts of retributive justice.

For some reason or other Adam and the boys never seemed to enter into his plans in that whole-souled way which he would have liked. They dampened his enthusiasm, and, as he frequently thought, he never felt so much like a captain as when he was captain of himself.

When the two young men with the keg disappeared among the bushes in the path which led to the spring—for this was one of the regular camping-places on the river—one of those bright ideas to which Chap was subject popped into his mind.

Gently taking down a double-barrelled gun, loaded with buckshot, from the hooks in the cabin on which it hung, and moving very cautiously so as not to awaken his companions, he stepped out on the sand.

He wore nothing but shirt and trousers, and, rolling up the latter, he ran along the beach to the Maggie, waded out to her, and got on board. Then, with his gun still in his hand, he slipped into the little cabin, where he crouched on his hands and knees.

There was a curtain at the open end of the cabin, and Chap drew this in front of him, so as to better conceal himself, leaving open a little crack through which he might peep.

He had conceived the plan of remaining here

until the two young men had reappeared, and were about to come on board. Then he would suddenly bounce out, and with loaded and cocked gun in hand, he would stop them just where they stood, and then he would give them a piece of his mind, and they should not move backward nor forward until he had said all he had to say.

They had taken possession of his boat, and he would take possession of theirs, and they should not have it again until he chose to give it to them.

Not another step should they take in their sneaking and nefarious career while it was his pleasure that they should stand and listen to him. This would be some satisfaction for the wrong he had sustained at their hands.

It seemed to the waiting Chap that the young men stayed away a very long time, but at last they reappeared, bearing the keg between them. But they did not act exactly as Chap desired.

One of them took the keg on his shoulder, while the other walked toward the bow of the boat. They thus became separated, and Chap could not yet carry out his plans. He must have them together so that he could cover them both with his gun. He could not deliver a lecture to one while the other was creeping up behind him. So he did not immediately rush out.

In the mean time, the man with the keg put his

burden on board, and stepped in himself. The other one got on the bow, and pulled the boat out toward the anchor, which was in deeper water. In doing this he turned the Maggie around, so that the stern was toward The Rolling Stone, the occupants of which were still sound asleep.

The man at the bow having pulled the anchor on board, stepped aft, and the two stood together for a moment on the stern, looking at the other boat. As they did so, Chap heard them make some derogatory remarks about the fellows who had taken their guns, and then one of them, with a low, disagreeable laugh, said he wondered what had become of the long-legged fellow they had chucked overboard.

This remark made Chap grind his teeth with anger. He would show them what had become of the long-legged fellow!

A desire for immediate vengeance possessed his whole being, and a plan of action flashed into his mind. Laying down his gun, and softly pushing aside the curtain, he made one wild bound directly at the two men, striking each of them in the middle of the back with his outstretched hands.

So sudden and tremendous was the unexpected push, that each of the fellows bent forward, tripped over the gunwale, and went head-foremost into the river, the boat being now in about four feet of water.

"Crouch down there, you varlets!"

Chap sprang instantly for his gun, and by the time the two dripping and astounded faces arose from the water, he was standing on the stern with his double-barrelled weapon cocked and pointed at them.

"Aha!" he cried; "now you know where that long-legged fellow is! And now perhaps you know how it feels to be chucked into the water. Crouch down there, you varlets!" he shouted, as one of them began to move toward the shore. "If you stir from where you are, or lift your chins out of water, I'll fire into you."

The two fellows, pale, frightened, and trembling, crouched down, with their mouths just above the surface of the water, while the fiery Chap told them what he thought of them.

"You're a pretty couple of sneaks to come along, two to one, and pitch into a fellow who treated you as if you were decent human beings, and then steal everything he has, and leave him alone to starve or,"—he was going to add, "or freeze to death," but remembering that this would not be possible in that climate, he said,—"or perish in any way he thought best. You didn't care what became of him. I'm not going to tell you the trouble you caused the rest of the party, but if ever two wild beasts deserve to be shot, you do."

Chap's face now glowed with such righteous indignation that one of the young men piteously begged him not to point that cocked gun at them, for it might go off.

"Go off!" cried Chap, without moving the weapon. "It would serve you right if it did go off, and put an end to your lives of crime. Such creatures as you are not needed in this world any more than snakes or alligators."

This last word seemed to instinctively affect one of the men, who, turning his eyes riverward, saw, or thought he saw, something dark moving along in the deep water beyond. Seized by a new fear, he raised himself and made a step toward shore.

Without a second's hesitation Chap pointed his gun a few feet above the fellow's head and fired; and at the instant of the report both heads disappeared beneath the surface of the water.

The sound of Chap's voice, when he was haranguing the two men in the water, aroused the occupants of the other boat, and Phil, Phœnix, and Adam were soon popping up their heads to see what Chap was about.

"Hello!" cried Phœnix, "he is on a boat over there talking like wildfire."

"I believe he is preaching to a pair of turtles!" cried Phil.

"Look here," said Adam, with alarm in his countenance, "there's something up. Slip on some clothes, and let's get over there. That's the Maggie, and he's got them two fellers in the water."

"What on earth does it mean?" asked Phil.

"Haven't the least idea," said Adam, "but we must——"

At this moment the report of Chap's gun rung through the air, and Adam and the two boys, barefooted and partially dressed, did not wait for another instant, but sprang from the boat and ran for the scene of commotion.

The wind had gradually blown the Maggie landward, and she was now grounded in very shallow water.

Chap still stood upon the stern, with his gun pointed to the two men, who, having held their heads under water until their faces were nearly black with suffocation, had now raised themselves, and were begging piteously that Chap would put down that gun and let them out. But the relentless Chap was just beginning a fresh series of denunciations, when Adam sprang on board of the Maggie, and, seizing his arm, threw up the muzzle of the gun.

"What on earth are you about?" cried the astonished sailor. "Are you goin' to kill 'em?"

"No," said Chap, coolly; "I haven't any idea of killing them. I only wanted to soak some of the wickedness out of them."

" Well, I reckon they're soaked about enough," said Adam.

" All right!" said Chap, with a grand air. "You have my permission to come out now, and I have nothing more to say to you.   I think you understand by this time what sort of an opinion I have of you."

And, so saying, he shouldered his gun, and went ashore, where, joining the two boys, he gave them an account of the adventure, which they received with shouts of laughter.

" Now, then," said Adam to the two dripping men, who had climbed on the deck of the Maggie, " you had better put on some dry clothes, and get out of this as quick as you can.   I don't want to see you shot; but you've done enough to that young man to warrant him in gettin' any kind o' satisfaction out o' you, short o' killin', and I don't know what he may take it into his head to do next.   I s'pose you put in here for water."

The young men were dragging some old trousers and shirts from under their bunks, and while one of them surlily remarked that they had got their water, and did not want to stay there any longer, the other made an earnest appeal to have their guns restored to them.

" Not much!" said Adam.   "I wouldn't trust you with 'em afore, and I guess you're in a worse temper now than you were when I took 'em.

We'll leave the guns at the hotel in Titusville, and you can go there and git 'em; and that's all I have to say about it."

And, with this remark, Adam left the Maggie, which in ten minutes more had pushed off and was sailing away.

16

CHAPTER XIX.

WAITING FOR A VISITOR.

DURING the rest of that day The Rolling Stone had a fair wind, and made a good trip. An hour after starting she passed the Maggie, which kept well away on the other side of the river. Evening was coming on, when Adam ran his boat in at a point he had been very anxious to make. This was at a solitary little house, at the edge of the woods, inhabited by a man whom he knew. During his former life on the Indian River, Adam had made the acquaintance of nearly all the settlers along the shores, and he was delighted to find that his old friend, Tom Pitman, still lived at this place.

Pitman was a tall, wiry man, full of action, and very talkative. He had a small house near the shore, where he lived, with his wife and two half-grown daughters, and, back in the woods, he

182

had cleared a field, which he had planted with pine-apples.

Everything about the place seemed neat and in good order. The field and a small yard in front of the house were well fenced, and there was a little pier running out into the water, near which a small boat was moored, while a sail-boat was in course of repair on the beach near by.

Pitman came out of his house as The Rolling Stone sailed up, and gave Adam and his companions a hearty welcome; but, in spite of his cheerful manner, Adam noticed that there seemed to be something on his mind. He was continually looking about him, and seemed to be in a great hurry to get the party disposed of for the night.

"I suppose we can tie up to your pier, Tom?" said Adam.

"I don't know about that," replied Pitman; "not if any of you is goin' to sleep on board. I'd have you all come up and sleep in the house, but I haven't got room enough for four of you. I've got a bed, though, that two of you can have. But them that sleeps on the boat had better anchor out a good ways from the shore, after we've all had our supper, and it's dark. You needn't do no cookin' for yourselves. You've all got to come in-doors, and eat with us."

"I suppose we can tie up here till supper is over, can't we?" asked Adam.

"Well, no," said Pitman, a little nervously. "You'd better run her up on the beach there by my boat, and bring your anchor ashore. It may be dark afore we've done supper."

"What's up?" asked Adam. "Anything partic'lar?"

"Well, yes," said Pitman, lowering his voice. "Is these young friends o' yourn scary?"

"Can't say that they are," said Adam. "You can tell 'em anything you can tell me."

"Well, then," said Pitman, "I'll tell just how 'tis. I didn't want to frighten these young men, for I s'posed, from their looks, that they'd come down from the North, and weren't used to the kind o' things that turn up in these wild parts. But if you say go ahead, all right. Last night a big painter came out o' the woods, and went out on that pier. My dog seed him out there, and made for him. I didn't know anything about it till I heard the noise o' the fight, and then I came out with my gun; but afore I could git here the painter had killed the dog, and had dragged him a good way up the shore. I got sight o' him, and blazed away. I reckon I didn't hit him, but he just left the dog, and put into the woods. Painters is cowards when there's a man about, but they ain't afeard o' no dog. Now, it's my 'pinion that that beast'll be back on that pier to-night, hopin' he'll git hold of another dog, and I'm goin' to watch for him. Now, you can see for yourselves that it wouldn't be exactly pleasant to be sleepin' in a boat at the foot of that pier with a big painter standin' and lookin' down at you, and makin' up his mind whether he should go aboard or not."

"No, indeed!" said Adam; "not even if you were waitin' with your rifle ready, Tom."

"I reckon he'd be worse company," said Pitman, "after I'd hit him than before, if I didn't kill him out and out."

"If you are going to watch for a panther," cried Chap, "I'm sure none of us will want to go to bed, either in the boat or the house. We've got guns along, and why can't we all have the fun of hunting the beast?"

"It don't do to have too many for that sort of thing," said Pitman; "but if any o' you want to jine in the sport, I'm willin'. It'll make us more certain of gittin' him. And now let's go in and have supper as quick as we can. Then we'll come out and make things ready for the varmint."

It was all very well for Mr. Pitman to talk about having supper soon, but his wife and two daughters, who had to prepare the meal for four additional persons, and all of them very hungry, found it no easy matter to get through with their cooking as rapidly as the head of the family desired.

It was no use for Mr. Pitman to say that if they didn't hurry the painter would come for his supper before they were through with their own. His wife only answered that she reckoned the painter could wait, and went on with her frying and stewing.

At last they all sat down to the usual cornbread, coffee, and fried ham, with the addition of a great dish of stewed oysters.

The boys had eaten some of the oysters, which are found in vast beds in parts of the Indian River, but had not found them much to their liking. They seemed fresher and more insipid than those to which they had been accustomed. But these were cooked so nicely that they ate them with great delight, and, altogether, they made the best meal they had had since leaving home.

Mr. Pitman was very nervous during the meal, and thought his guests would never be done eating. He did not begrudge them their food, but he was full of anxiety lest the panther should come and go before they had made themselves ready to receive his visit.

When Phœnix and Chap had eaten their last mouthful, and Adam had drained the third cup of coffee, Mr. Pitman put back his chair, and the party arose. Adam greatly desired to smoke his evening pipe, but to this his host decidedly objected.

"There won't be time," he said, "and besides, the critter might smell the smoke. Better wait till we're through with this business, and then you can smoke all you like."

Adam good-naturedly assented to this arrangement, and the male members of the party went outside, while Mrs. Pitman and daughters were cautioned to keep in the house, and shut the doors and lower windows, for if the panther should be brought to bay, he might think the house a good place of refuge.

Mr. Pitman took upon himself the whole plan of arrangement. He first examined the arms of the party. He himself had a rifle.

One of the guns taken from the Maggie was a breech-loading rifle, and it was loaded, but there were no extra cartridges to fit it, and only one shot could be fired from it. This was given to Adam.

The other gun, belonging to the two young men, was a small shot-gun, one barrel of which had been discharged that morning by Chap. Both barrels were now loaded with number two shot, but Mr. Pitman declared the weapon altogether unserviceable for work of the kind expected.

"It won't carry far enough," he said, "and the shot will scatter. A painter wouldn't take into no account—a gun like that."

The double-barrelled gun, which had been hired

from Mr. Brewer, was loaded with buck-shot, and this, Pitman considered, might be of some service, and it was given to Phil, as he was the best shot among the boys.

"As for you two other young men," said Mr. Pitman, "the best thing you can do is to get into your boat and anchor her a little way out in the river. You can see the sport from there as well as anywhere, if you can see it at all; and if there's too many folks ashore, I'm afraid the painter will smell us out, or see somebody; and besides, I wouldn't want to have him ranging 'round here, and two young fellows in the bushes with no way to take care of themselves."

Chap and Phœnix did not like this plan very much, but they preferred being in the boat to going into the house and peeping through a crack.

It was lighter on the water than on the land, and Mr. Pitman assured them that if they kept themselves pretty much out of sight, and quiet, they could look all they liked, for the panther wouldn't mind a boat, for there had been boats around when he came the night before.

So Chap and Phœnix went on board The Rolling Stone, taking the smaller shot-gun with them, and, pushing out a couple of hundred feet from shore, anchored and lay down to await events.

Adam and Phil were then placed behind some

low-growing bushes a little distance up the beach ; while Mr. Pitman took his position behind the roots of a fallen palmetto, not far away.

The panther was expected to come from the woods below the house, and from their places of concealment each of the party could get a good view of the little pier where the dog had been killed, and which was still stained with his blood.

The wind was blowing gently from the south, so that if the panther carried out the plan as Mr. Pitman had arranged it, there would be no danger of his catching the scent of his concealed enemies.

CHAPTER XX.

THE VISITOR ARRIVES.

For a long, long time our friends behind the bushes and the uprooted tree, as well as those in the boat, waited and waited for the appearance of the panther.

It was now as dark as it would be, but the stars were out, and, with eyes accustomed to the gloom, objects could be easily seen upon the beach or on the water.

But, so far, nothing moved from the woods toward the little pier.

"I might just as well have had another cup of coffee," whispered Adam, "for there was plenty in the pot, and have smoked my pipe. I knowed he'd be a long time comin'."

"You mustn't talk so much," said Mr. Pitman, from his post near by, "for painters have mighty sharp ears. And mind, I don't want any of you to fire till he's out on the pier, for if you crack at him while he's on the beach, you might send a ball into the house. That 'ud make it lively for mother and the girls. I put us all here close together, so that we shouldn't fire into one another."

"Who's talking now?" thought Phil, but he said nothing.

"Phœnix," said Chap, after the two had watched and watched and watched, "I don't believe much in this panther business, after all. I move that you and I take regular watches like the sailors on a ship. First, one of us can take a nap for half an hour, and then he can wake up and let the other one have a snooze for the same time. In this way each of us can get half a night's sleep in broken dozes. As for that panther, he's badly behind time; most likely switched off on a siding to let a down train, such as a couple of bears, pass him."

Phœnix agreed to this proposal, and kindly allowed Chap to take the first nap.

At the end of what he supposed was a good half-hour, but which was, in reality, only twenty minutes, Phœnix tried to wake up his companion; but it was of no use. Chap slept as sound as a log, and he could not be aroused, unless more noise and confusion were made than would be proper on such an occasion. So Phœnix determined to watch a little longer, and if nothing turned up, to go to sleep himself.

Just about the time this resolution was made, Mr. Pitman remarked, in a very audible whisper, that if he had had a puppy dog, that he did not care much about, he would have tied it to the end of the pier, and then its yelping would have attracted the panther's attention, and he would have been certain to go out there to get it.

Phil whispered that he thought that would have been a cruel thing to do.

"Oh, no," replied Mr. Pitman. "There wouldn't 'a' been no danger to the dog. I'd 'a' put a ball through the painter afore he'd got to him. Stop talking! Look thar!"

There was no occasion to tell anybody to look, for along the beach, not very far from the edge of the woods, a dark form, like that of an immense cat, was moving, stealthily, but with moderate speed, toward the house and the pier.

Phil trembled in every fibre when he saw this creature, not with fear, but with excitement.

"Is that a panther?" he thought. "So near a house, and right on the very beach where we are ourselves?"

He raised his gun a little in imitation of Adam, who was kneeling silently behind his bush; but his arms trembled so much that he thought he would never be able to hit anything, no matter how near it might be.

Phœnix also saw the approaching panther, and

all idea of sleep immediately forsook him. He endeavored to gently arouse Chap, but this was useless, and with strained eyes he watched the scene on shore.

The panther, as it came up the beach, passed so near to the house that even Mr. Pitman was amazed, and thought that he would not have slept so soundly during the many nights he had spent in that house, if he had known that a panther would dare to prowl so near its windows. But this beast was unusually rash or courageous, and it is seldom indeed that a panther will venture so near a human habitation; but among wild animals, as well as men, there are individuals who are more daring and reckless of consequences than their fellows; and in the wilder parts of Florida, panthers of an investigating or enterprising turn of mind have been known to totally disregard the proximity of man.

When nearly opposite the little gate of the house-yard, the panther stopped, and raised its head as if listening, and then, with a noiseless trot, it went directly toward the place where it had killed the dog. It walked more slowly along the pier, putting down its head occasionally to sniff, and then stopped upon the extreme end of the little platform, its small head and long, lithe body standing out clearly against the sky.

At this moment the reports of two rifles, sounding almost like one, rang out upon the night, while immediately after them the two barrels of a heavily-loaded shot-gun were discharged with a heavier and more resounding detonation.

Almost at the instant of the rifle-shots, and an instant perhaps before Phil fired, the panther sprang into the air, and came down, not upon the pier, but into the water beyond. There was a great splash, and then he could be plainly seen swimming away from shore.

Phil, Adam, and Pitman sprang out of their concealment, and the latter hastily reloaded his rifle.

It was probable that the panther had been struck, for it was scarcely to be supposed that the mere noise of the reports would have frightened him so much that he would have taken to the water, but he could not have been badly hurt, for he was swimming vigorously.

At first it seemed as if the panther was making for the other side of the river, but he had not swum out very far before he changed his course, and made directly for The Rolling Stone.

At the moment he turned, Pitman's rifle again rang out, and the ball was seen to send up a quick jet of water a yard or two beyond the swimming animal.

The situation was now an alarming one. Phil was reloading, and Pitman already had another charge in his rifle; but it was impossible now to fire at the panther without aiming directly at the boat. Adam dropped his rifle, and ran toward the small boat by the beach. He would have rowed out to do what he could to help the boys, despite the danger to himself, but there was no oars in the boat.

"Push off! push off!" shouted Pitman to the boys in the boat. "Pull up your anchor! Haul up your sail!"

He evidently thought that the only means of safety was to sail away from the panther as soon as possible.

But there was no time for all this to be done, even if Phœnix and Chap had been expert in the management of anchors and sails, which they were not. The panther was evidently making for The Rolling Stone as a place of refuge, and from the way he was swimming he would quickly reach it. He seemed to totally disregard the presence of two boys on board, or the fact had escaped his attention.

The sound of the firing had, of course, awakened Chap, and he and Phœnix were hastily discussing what they should do. Phœnix seized a hatchet, and posted himself by the side of the boat.

"If he comes near, I'll brain him," said he.

Chap snatched up the shot-gun. It had been

pronounced harmless to panthers, but it might frighten the brute.

The panther was now within four or five feet of the boat, and Phœnix stood ready, with his hatchet raised. Chap kneeled down, and leaned over the boatside, and as he did so, he involuntarily reached out his gun toward the panther. This action seemed to irritate the beast, and he was so near that he actually opened his mouth, and took hold of the muzzle of the gun. At this instant Chap pulled both triggers, and two loads of number two shot, in almost compact masses, entered the panther's brain. When the boys looked at the water, there was nothing but a swirl of ripples where the angry head had just been seen.

"You've settled him!" cried Phœnix; but still he stood ready with his uplifted hatchet.

In a moment the body of the panther reappeared, now nearer the boat, one side uppermost, limp and motionless.

"He's dead!" cried Chap. "Grab him! Don't let him sink again!"

And, throwing down the gun, he leaned over the side of the boat.

"Look out!" cried Phœnix. "If he isn't dead, it won't be much fun to grab him."

CHAPTER XXI.

THE METROPOLIS OF THE INDIAN RIVER.

Phil, Adam, and Mr. Pitman had been standing on the shore, watching with breathless anxiety the rapid course of the events recorded in the previous chapter. As the panther neared the boat, they were almost wild with terror, but they could offer no help, and the two boys seemed to be doing all that could be done.

Their eyes were now so accustomed to the obscurity of the night, and there was so much reflected starlight from the water, that they could plainly see the panther's head as it swam, and Phœnix's form was very distinct as he stood with uplifted hatchet.

They saw that Chap had the gun, and each in his heart hoped that he might fire it and frighten away the beast.

When the gun was fired, and the triumphant

cries of the boys were heard, Adam shouted across the water,—

"Look out! he'll be at you again!"

The good sailor had no idea anything had happened, but that the panther had been frightened away by the discharge of the gun. The dark reflection of the boat made it impossible for him to see what was going on in the water close to its side.

Chap, however, was not to be discouraged by Adam's shout or Phœnix's warning.

"The thing is dead!" he cried, "and I'm not going to lose it. It'll sink again before you know it. There's its tail close to you. Can't you take hold of it?"

Phœnix hesitated. To take hold of the tail of a wild beast which a minute before had been full of angry life, seemed to him a risky piece of business. The animal might be merely stunned, and, reviving, might object to have its tail pulled. Still, Phœnix was as loath as Chap to lose the panther, and as the body seemed about to sink again he reached out and seized the floating tail.

Chap was so excited that he would have gladly clutched the panther by the back of the neck, but it was just a little out of his reach.

Phœnix pulled the tail toward him, and Chap sprang to assist.

"It's dead! it's dead!" yelled Chap, as the two

boys pulled steadily at the tail, and the motionless body of the panther was drawn close to the boat.

When Phil and the two men heard Chap cry that the panther was dead, they were as much amazed as relieved. They had not supposed the shot they had heard could have killed the beast. They were now anxious to get to the spot as quickly as possible, and see what had really happened.

Pitman ran into the house, and came back with the oars, and followed by his wife and daughters, who, now that they heard the panther was dead, were perfectly willing to come out of doors, and stood on the beach while Mr. Pitman, Adam, and Phil jumped into the boat, and rapidly rowed to The Rolling Stone.

When they reached her side, they found Phœnix and Chap each having hold of one of the hind legs of the panther, and pulling it into the boat.

A lantern was lighted, and the beast carefully examined. It was a handsome, full-grown panther, as big a one, Mr. Pitman said, as he had ever seen.

When the manner of the killing had been fully explained, and it had been found that the panther had been struck in the leg by one rifle ball, although of course, it could not be determined from whose rifle it came, Chap stood up and leaned against the cabin, the light of the lantern shining full upon his manly form.

"Gentlemen," said he, affecting a portly grandeur, while his eyes twinkled good-humoredly, "if you want to know how to kill a panther, or any other beast, come to me, and I'll tell you how to do it. It's all nonsense to double yourself up for hours behind a prickly palmetto bush, and sit there till your back aches, and wishing you had never heard of the thing, and were comfortable in bed. You might just as well lie down and take a comfortable sleep, and then when the wild beast comes up to you, just wake up and poke your gun into his mouth, and blow his brains out. That is the easy and sensible way of doing the thing with all the modern improvements."

"All very fine," laughed Phil, "if you have somebody to wake you up at the proper moment, and drive the panther to the place where you are snoozing."

"Of course, of course!" said Chap, with a grand wave of his hand. "The captain must have his retainers; that is understood."

The panther was put into the small boat, and Adam and Pitman rowed ashore.

There the dead beast, after having been viewed with much delight by the female Pitmans, was hung up to the limb of a tree and carefully skinned by the two men.

When this job was finished Adam was glad to accept his friend's offer of a bed, the three boys being, by this time, fast asleep on their boat.

After breakfast, the next morning, Mr. Pitman asked Chap for his address, and informed him that after he had properly prepared the skin of the panther, he intended to send it to him.

To this Chap demurred, saying that Mr. Pitman ought to keep the skin himself, and if he gave it to anybody, he ought to give it to some one of the party who had had so long and weary a watch for it, and not to the fellow who had gone to sleep and let the rest look out for the approach of the beast.

But Mr. Pitman would listen to nothing of the kind, insisting that the one who shot the panther should have the skin, and Phil, Phœnix, and Adam agreeing that this was right, the matter was so settled.

As soon as possible our party set sail, with hearty expressions of good-will toward the Pitman family. The wind was fair, and, after a stop that night at a place where nothing memorable occurred, they came early the next afternoon in sight of Titusville.

On the way much attention had been paid to the health and comfort of the little bears, and now that they were nearing the town, Adam gave the tiller to Phil, and began to comb the soft hair and to generally tidy up the little cubs. One of these animals had such a wise air that Phil named him Solomon, whereupon Chap declared that his little sister should be called the Queen of Sheba, giving a very broad sound to the final "a," in imitation of the backwoods accent.

"If there's anybody in the town," said Adam, "that wants 'em bad enough to pay well for 'em, I'll let 'em have 'em; but if no such person turns up, I'll lug the little creturs North as long as I've money enough to buy milk."

"Is this what that girl in the woods considered a big place?" exclaimed Chap, as they sailed up to the town. "What would she say if she saw the mighty metropolis of Boontown, not to mention New York, London, or Pekin?"

Titusville was a settlement of about thirty or forty low wooden houses, none of them far from the river-front, and all seeming to cluster around and to depend upon an extensive one-story building, forming three sides of a square, and fronted by large and well-kept grounds, which stretched for two or three hundred feet to the river, where there was a pretty little wharf. This house was the hotel, and the only building of any size or pretension in the place.

As they came up to the wharf, they saw sitting on the extreme end of the platform a small man, with sandy hair, short trousers, no stockings, and cowhide shoes.

"I'll bet the left ear of little Solomon," said Adam, "that that's the brother of John Brewer. There's a kind o' family likeness about him."

The little man helped them to make the boat fast, and as he did so a smile of recognition seemed to flicker over his face.

"Are you John Brewer's brother?" said Adam, when he landed.

"Yes," said the other. "And that's his boat, ain't it?"

Adam replied that it was, and explained the arrangement that had been made.

"I've been a-waitin' here for the mail-boat," said the other, bringing out his words very slowly, "but now that this one's here, I reckon I may as well take her."

"Don't you think you'd a great sight better take her?" said Adam. "I consider this a tip-top chance for you to get back comfortable and save money."

"I reckon that's so," said the other. "Goin' up to the hotel?"

"Yes," said Adam, "and if you'll come along, we'll give you the money that we owe your brother, —that is, if the treasurer says so."

"All right," said Phœnix.

And after making the boat secure, the valises and other traps were taken out, and the whole party walked up the broad, gravel path which led to the hotel.

CHAPTER XXII.

THE COLONEL.

As the party approached the hotel, they saw on the wide porch which ran along the front of the main building a man in a wheeled chair.

"That's the colonel," said Adam. "He owns the hotel and pretty much the whole town besides."

"He's in an invalid's chair," remarked Phil; "but he don't look very sick."

"Sick!" laughed Adam. "Not much! But he's been in that chair a long time."

They now reached the porch and ascended the steps.

The colonel, who had been steadfastly watching them as they came up the path, was a heavy, vigorous-looking man, broad-chested, and sun-burned, with a clear, piercing eye and a powerful voice. One of his feet was affected by chronic rheumatism, and thus being unable to walk, he spent all his waking time in his wheeled chair, in which he moved about the premises, sometimes turning the wheels himself, and sometimes being pushed by a servant.

At meal times he was wheeled to the head of the table; when business was to be attended to, he was rolled to the clerk's desk, and wherever he was needed, there he and his chair were sure to be found.

He had been a pioneer and a soldier in his time, and had been noted for his great energy and high spirit.

These qualities, which had once made him conspicuous in border warfare, and had carried him through many dangers, both by land and sea, had now made him the master spirit of this little settlement on the Indian River. He had projected the settlement; owned the greater part of it; held its principal offices, and exercised a general power, which resembled that of an ancient baron over his feudal subjects.

"Well, Adam Guy," said the colonel, extending his hand to the sailor, "where did you come from? and who have you brought with you? I don't mean Sam Brewer. I know all I want to know about him."

Adam then introduced the three boys, and proposed that Phil, whom he seemed to consider the

18

best talker of the party, should tell how it happened
that they were there.

Wooden chairs, which were abundant on the
porch, were now drawn up, and Phil told the
story of the adventures of himself and his companions from the time of the wreck of the tug-
boat up to the present moment, leaving out, of
course, many incidents, which, although interesting,
were not necessary to be told.

The colonel listened, fixing his keen eyes on
Phil all the time that he was telling his story.

"Well," said he, "you've had a pretty rough
time of it, but you've got to a safe port at last.
I suppose you want to go on North as soon as you
can, hey?"

"Oh, yes," said Phil; "our friends must be
very anxious about us, and we want to get to them
as soon as possible."

"No doubt of it," said the colonel. "I've heard
about you, and I've been looking out for you for
three or four days. You've been a precious long
time getting up the river. Doctor Walker told me
about you—saw you down at Brewer's—and he
had a message for your folks which he was going
to telegraph when he got to Sanford."

"I suppose he has sent the telegram by this
time," said Phil.

"Oh, yes," replied the colonel. "He got here
the middle of the week, caught the boat, and went

right on. But you fellows will have to stay here till Wednesday. There won't be no boat till then."

The boys looked at each other in consternation. This was Saturday, and a delay of three days in this place seemed a grievous thing to them.

"You needn't look so long-faced about it!" exclaimed the colonel. "You can't go on, and you might as well be satisfied. Here's a good hotel, where you can be comfortable and live well at a reasonable price. You got safe to my place, and you're all right. When the time comes I'll start you off and fix everything straight for you. You needn't give yourselves any more trouble about anything. You couldn't be in a better place than this. Here's the finest air, the best accommodations, and the prettiest stretch of water in all Florida. All you've got to do is to enjoy yourselves. If you want to know anything, just come to me.—Bob!"

At this last word, which was shouted in a stentorian voice, a well-dressed negro boy came running to the colonel.

"Bob," said he, "take this party to Number six and Number seven,—two in one room and two in the other.—Now, you'd better go and fix yourselves up. Supper will be ready in half an hour."

When the boys had washed and dressed themselves and put on the white shirts they had brought in their valises, they looked quite neat and presentable, while Adam, who shared Phœnix's room, —for this establishment was conducted on democratic principles,—came in afterward, and put himself into the best order possible, combing and curling his hair as carefully as if he had been an old-time dandy.

When the boys went into the large central room of the hotel, they found the colonel at his desk, for he was his own clerk, and they entered their names on the register.

"What are your charges, colonel?" asked Phœnix, who was the last one at the desk.

"Our regular charge is two dollars and a half a day," said the colonel, "but I'll take you four for nine dollars a day."

Phœnix made no answer, but for a moment his face seemed almost as long as Chap's legs. Supper was now ready, and during the first part of the meal Phœnix said but little, and seemed to have no appetite; but the example of his companions soon had an effect upon him, and he began to eat as heartily as anybody.

"This is a tip-top place," said Chap, as the three boys walked down the gravelled path after supper. "I don't know when I've eaten such a gorgeous meal."

"The meal is gorgeous enough," said Phœnix, in a doleful tone, "but that isn't all of it. The price is a great sight more gorgeous. What do you say to nine dollars a day for the four of us?"

"Nine dollars!" exclaimed Chap. "We can't do anything like that. We haven't got money enough, have we? After we've paid for the boat, we won't begin to have enough."

"We must go to some cheaper place," said Phil. "Of course we can't pay such rates as that."

Adam and Brewer now joined the party, and as the identity of the latter had been established, he was paid the eight dollars that was due for the hire of the boat and the gun. He said he did not intend to start down the river that night, but further than this he seemed to have no plans, and strolled down toward the river.

"Adam," said Phil, "we must get out of this place. It is too expensive for us. Where shall we find the cheapest kind of a hotel or boarding-house?"

Adam laughed.

"You can't find it in this town," he said. "If you want to stop in Titusville, you've got to stop in this house. There isn't any other place to go to. Catch any of the people of this town takin' boarders away from the colonel! They know better what's good for 'em."

"But what are we to do?" asked Phœnix. "We haven't got the money to stay here."

"Well," said Adam, "I've very little money with me, but if I had it I'd lend it to you. But you needn't bother yourselves about me. I can work my way North somehow."

"No, that won't do," said Phil. "You know we told you that if you'd sail our boat, and show us the way, and do all those things that we don't know anything about, we'd pay your way North, and we'll do it, too, as soon as we get money from our friends. But the thing is, what are we to do now? We've used more than we expected to, and we didn't suppose there would be hotel bills here. We thought we'd go right on."

"Well, now I'll tell you," said Adam, "what you'd better do. Just go, all three of you, to the colonel, and tell him the fix you're in. It's his business to set things right in this town, and he'll let you know what you have to do. If anything is to be set up or knocked down, he wants to do it himself."

"I'm not particularly anxious to have him knock me down," said Chap.

"It'll go easier to be knocked down now" said Adam, "than after you've run up a great big bill, and I recommend you to go straight to him, and let him know how things stand."

CHAPTER XXIII.

A NEW EXPEDITION PLANNED.

THE boys went up to the hotel, where they found the colonel sitting behind his desk.

Phil was generally expected to do the talking for the party whenever anything important was to be said, and he, therefore, with very little preface or hesitation, informed the big man in the chair of the condition in which he and his friends now found themselves in regard to finances.

The colonel listened to what Phil told him, and then, after looking at them all with a steady glance, he said :

"Got no money, hey?"

The boys wished he would not speak so loud and clear, for there were several persons in the room, and Phœnix answered,—

"We've got some, but not enough."

"How much have you got?" asked the colonel.

The treasurer then explained that, owing to their having been very long on the way, and also having to pay more for boat-hire, food, etc., than they had expected, and to hire Indians, they had only about seventeen dollars left. They had hoped to have enough to take them to Enterprise or Sanford, where Adam thought that some of the steamboat captains would take them on board, and let them pay for their passage when they got to Jacksonville.

"I don't believe they'd do it," said the colonel. "They're too sharp for that sort of thing. You haven't enough to pay your way from here anywhere, or to stay here. Are you sure of money when you get to Jacksonville?"

"Oh, yes," said Phil, promptly. "If that telegram was sent on I expect there are funds waiting there for us now, and if there isn't, or if there shouldn't be enough, we'll telegraph, and they'll send us all we need."

The colonel rubbed his head.

"Well," said he, "you can stay here till Wednesday, all four of you, for I suppose you still count Adam Guy in your party, and I'll make out your bill at my regular rates, and I'll make it out to you," pointing to Phil; "and when you get home—you needn't do it before—you can send me the amount."

The boys all looked relieved, and each one thanked the colonel heartily.

"That's all right," said he. "You're not the handsomest fellows I ever see, but you look honest."

A slight shade of anxiety now returned to Phœnix's face.

"How much will it cost, sir," he said, "to go from here to Enterprise?"

"I charge you a dollar apiece," said the colonel, "to carry you over to Salt Lake. That's seven miles away, and it's where you take the steamboat. Then the fare is six dollars apiece to Enterprise or Sanford."

"Squelched again!" said Chap.

The colonel looked at him with a half smile.

"A fellow with legs like yours," he said, "ought to be able to walk it. The soft spots you'd have to pass over ain't more'n a yard deep."

"Oh, *I* could walk it easy enough," said Chap; "but I couldn't carry three short-legged fellows. That's where the trouble comes in."

"Well, then, I guess I won't make you do it," said the colonel. "Let me see," taking a pencil and a piece of paper; "four ones is four, and four sixes is twenty-four, and then four more sixes, from Sanford to Jacksonville, is twenty-four more, and then a couple of dollars for extras—none of you fellows drink, do you?"

"Not one of us," promptly replied Chap.

"I thought as much," said the colonel, "and that comes to fifty-four dollars. Take seventeen from that, and it leaves thirty-seven. That's the amount you are short, and, to make it even, we'll call it forty. Now, if one of you fellows will make out a note to me for forty dollars, payable in thirty days, and the other two will indorse it, I'll let you have the money."

This unexpected offer almost stupefied the boys, and they could scarcely find words with which to express their gratitude.

"Oh, it'll be all right enough," said the colonel. "I know that all of you or one of you will pay me the money, or I'll make it hot for you, no matter what part of the country you're in. When a man owes me money, he pays it."

"But none of us are of age," suggested Phil. "Perhaps our signatures——"

"Don't talk to me of age," roared the colonel. "If I lend you the money, you'll pay it back to me. There'll be no getting out of that. I won't charge you any interest. It'll be cheaper for me to let that money go for awhile without bringing in anything than to keep you fellows here eating at the rate of four dollars a day a head."

When Adam was told of the arrangement which had been made between the colonel and the boys, he smiled.

"You might travel a long ways," he said, "be-

fore you'd come across such another man as the
colonel. If you treat him square and he likes you,
he's ready at any time to give you a friendly h'ist;
but if you get him down on you, you'll wish you'd
never been born. Nobody need think that because
the colonel is sittin' in that chair all day and can't
never walk a step out of it that he needn't be afraid
of him. When I was down here afore, he used to
have something to do with the revenue service, and
if he'd hear of any smugglers tryin' to get into the
country across this river with cigars or anything
else, he'd have his chair rolled in no time aboard
the boat he used to sail in, and he put after them
fellers, and I can tell you what it is, there's no
man that ever put in along this coast with smug-
gled goods would want to see the colonel comin'
after him, with his rifle in his hands, and that
black eye of his a-flashin' out about a mile ahead.
He always was an ugly customer to run afoul of,
and he's jist as bad now as ever, if things go crooked.
I ain't surprised a bit at what he did for you fellers.
It's jist like him."

The next day was Sunday, and the boys looked
so bright and fresh, with their well-blackened boots
and their clean white shirts and collars, that they
felt quite fit to mingle in general society.

They would have gone to church, but were prevented from so doing by the fact that the town did
not yet contain a church.

On Monday morning, after breakfast, the three boys were sitting in a small summer-house, which was built at the end of the pier belonging to the hotel.

A little way out in the river, The Rolling Stone was moored, and there were other boats anchored here and there in the river.

A party of sportsmen who had been at the hotel had already started on a trip down the river, and the white sails of their little yacht could be seen several miles away over the blue and sparkling water.

The river here was very broad, it being six miles across to the wide, low island which separated it from the sea, but for a long way out from the shore it was very shallow, and a party of boys with rolled-up trousers, waded out with their cast-nets to a distance which very much astonished our friends upon the pier.

"Well, I tell you what it is!" cried Chap; "we've got to do something, or go somewhere. We won't leave this town till Wednesday, and that gives us two clear days, and we don't want to waste them. Now, the point is, what is there to do that we can get the most fun out of?"

"I suppose Adam might put us up to something," said Phœnix, "but he's gone to work to help a man down there who is building a boat. He said he might as well make some money while he is here as not."

"Well, then we'll go ask some one else," said Chap. "We're bound to do something."

At this moment a slow step was heard on the pier, and Mr. Brewer's brother directly joined the group.

"Hello!" cried Chap. "I thought you would have been off for home long ago."

"No," said the other, languidly, taking a seat; "I ain't in no hurry. I reckon I'll start after awhile, some time. You fellers have got to wait here for the Winkyminky."

"What's that?" asked Phil.

"That's the boat you're goin' in on Wednesday," said Brewer's brother. "She's a good little boat—Cap'n Root's boat."

"I suppose that's the one," said Chap; "and we were just talking about what we should do while we were waiting for her. Can't you give us an idea? Would it pay to get a boat, and go out after ducks?"

"No," said the other; "that ain't much fun, and they ain't good eatin'. If I was you fellers, I'd go up to Lowper's Creek, and shoot 'gators."

"Shoot alligators!" cried Chap. "That's splendid! Where is that creek?"

"It's about ten or twelve miles above here," said Brewer's brother, "and it's jist chock full o' 'gators. You never see so many in all your born days. You kin hire a rifle at the hotel, and you kin git all the teeth and hides you want."

K 19

The boys considered this a glorious idea.

"But how will we get there?" asked Phil. "We might hire a boat, but Adam is busy, and couldn't sail us."

"I'll take you up in that boat," said Brewer, "and I kin sail you jist as well as Adam Guy. I won't charge you nothin', and I'll borrow a little dinky, and tow it behind. We have to go up the creek in a row-boat when we begin to hunt 'em."

All this promised great sport for the boys, and no time was lost in making the necessary arrangements.

It was planned that they should start as soon as possible, take some provisions along, stay up at the creek all night, and come back the next day.

When Adam heard of the scheme he at first looked a little doubtful, but then he smiled and said he reckoned the thing might work.

"But you'll have a gay time," he added, "goin' after 'gators with Coot Brewer."

"Coot?" asked Chap.

"Yes," said Adam; "that's the name he goes by along this river. I reckon he got it because he isn't good for much. But he ought to know how to sail a boat, and if you keep a sharp eye on him I guess he won't hender you much. I'd go along, but I can't back out of this job now."

CHAPTER XXIV.

COOT BREWER TAKES THE HELM.

THE boys did not start for Lowper's Creek and the alligators as soon as they expected. They found that a good deal of talk, and a good many preparations were necessary before they could get off.

The colonel did not altogether approve of the plan, but when he was assured that the boys could all swim, he said he reckoned no harm would come to them, and that they might as well be off on a trip of this kind as lounging around the hotel.

He called Bob, and gave orders than an abundance of provisions, enough to last the party till the following afternoon, should be immediately got ready. He also furnished them with a little oil-stove, on which to boil their coffee on board the boat.

"You see I'm not going to lose anything by your going up the creek," he said. "I'll keep your rooms for you, and furnish your meals. It'll cost you just as much, whether you sleep among the 'gators or among Christians."

The boys assured him that they had not the slightest idea of his making any reduction on account of the trip.

"I expect you fellows laugh," he said, "at my keeping you straight up to terms when I'm going to let you go away without paying me a red, but I do my business on a business basis. I don't give you anything, and I expect to get back all that's owing to me. Do you understand that?"

The boys understood it perfectly.

In the matter of hiring rifles, there was some little trouble. The colonel had but one, and there was no other rifle in the town at that time to be had excepting the weapon which, with a small shot-gun, had been captured from the men on board of the Maggie, and given to the colonel.

The latter had heard the story of the theft of The Rolling Stone, and had made no remark whatever on the subject, except that he would take charge of the guns, and keep them till they were called for.

Chap proposed that they should take this rifle, and pay the young men for the use of it, but this the colonel positively refused to allow. The gun had been hired in the town, and he would keep it until the persons who had taken it should appear.

So they were obliged to be content with but one rifle, although Brewer said that his brother's shot-gun, loaded with buckshot, would do as well for a 'gator as a bear, if they could only get near enough.

"What are you going to do with the 'gators you kill?" asked the colonel, when the boys were about to start.

"Oh, Mr. Brewer is going to prepare the skins and teeth of some of them, and send them on to us," said Phil.

"Do you hear that?" roared the colonel, to some men on the other side of the room. "Coot Brewer is going to polish the teeth and tan the hides of the 'gators these young men kill, and send them on to them at the North."

At this announcement there was a general laugh, during which the boys left.

"He thinks we can't kill alligators," said Chap; "but, then, all these people suppose we're city boys, just because we come from the North. I believe most folks down here have an idea that the whole North is built up solid with houses, like one great town, and it's no use telling them we've been using guns ever since we were big enough to hold them."

The Rolling Stone was found at the end of the pier, with Coot Brewer in it, and the row-boat which he had borrowed made fast to the stern. Adam was also there, having left his work to see them off.

"Be careful you don't shoot each other," was his parting injunction, "and don't haul in any 'gator till you're sure he's dead."

The boys agreed to remember these admonitions, and everything having been put aboard, The Rolling Stone set sail up the river, with a good wind almost directly from the south, which, as they were sailing northward, ought to have carried them rapidly along; but for some reason or other, the boat did not seem to behave as well as when Adam was at the helm.

Coot Brewer put her directly before the wind, and sometimes she would sail on at a good rate, and then she would begin to rock, the end of her boom almost dipping into the water as she went over on that side.

Phœnix had just remarked that the boat had never been so much like a rolling stone as now, when the motion became so violent that Brewer was a little frightened, and put her about so suddenly that the boom came round with tremendous force, just grazing the top of Chap's head.

"I should think that sort of thing would upset her," said Phil, who did not look upon Coot Brewer as much of a sailor.

"But it didn't, you see," remarked the helmsman, complacently. "She's a pretty stiff little boat."

After this, they tacked across the river for a while. Then they went before the wind again. Then they lay to while Mr. Brewer took in some reefs of the mainsail, which he said he would have done before had he thought about it.

"It'll make it easier for your heads," he said, "if she jibes."

After a sail which lasted a great deal longer than Mr. Brewer said it would, the boat arrived at the mouth of the creek.

"You can't sail up the creek, you know," said Brewer. "We go up there in the dinky. The way to hunt the 'gators here is to row up the creek a good long way, and then haul in oars and float down. That don't frighten 'em, you see, and you kin easy git near enough to shoot 'em. But it's too late to go up this evenin', and so we'd better anchor the boat, git our supper, and go to bed, so's to be up bright and airly to-morrow mornin'. We kin kill all the 'gators we want before noon, and then we'll have plenty of time to git back to town before it's dark."

This plan was agreed to, although the boys had hoped to begin their sport that afternoon, and the night was spent on the boat at the mouth of the creek.

"Do you hear 'em roarin' over there?" asked Mr. Brewer, after they had gone to bed. "I tell you we'll have splendid times to-morrow!"

CHAPTER XXV.

AMONG THE ALLIGATORS.

EARLY the next morning Chap awakened the party. The coffee was soon boiled, and after a hasty breakfast the two guns were put into the row-boat, together with some drinking water and a small luncheon, which Chap thought they might need, and Coot having taken the oars, they proceeded up the creek.

They had not gone very far before it became very evident that all that Coot Brewer had said about the alligators in that creek was entirely correct. The ugly creatures were seen in great numbers, appearing, as Chap said, to come from every direction except down from the sky. They rose up from the bottom of the creek, their great heads and backs appearing above the water.

The boat, which Coot rowed in an extremely gentle manner, did not seem to disturb them at all, and they came toward it, or swam away from it, as if it was of no consequence, some of them approaching almost within an oar's length. On the bank, huge monsters, who had been lying in the reeds and mud, raised themselves on their short legs, and looked around at the intruders, while big ones and little ones slumped into the water on each side, some of them swimming toward the boat, and some of them away from it.

"I'm going to take a crack at one of them," said Phil, picking up the rifle.

"No, no!" said Coot. "Don't do that. Wait till we float down."

"Why, we can't get a better chance than we have now," said Phil. "We don't frighten them a bit."

"But that ain't the way," said the other. "You've got to hunt 'em the right way, or it's no good."

So they rowed on still farther, and the creek became a little narrower, while the number of alligators greatly increased. Several times Coot touched one of them with the end of the oar, and a big fellow rose right under the boat, giving it quite a jar.

"Look here!" said Coot, with a troubled expression. "I never see 'em as thick as this afore. This warm weather has brought 'em out."

"We might as well shoot some of them," said Chap. "We can never have a better chance."

P

"Don't you do it," cried Coot. "You'll make 'em mad, and they'll pitch in and clean us up in less than no time."

"What's the good of coming," said Phil, "if we can't shoot them when we see them."

"Wait till we git where there ain't so many," said Coot. "I reckon they're scarcer higher up."

"Queer way of hunting," remarked Phœnix, "when you look for a place where the game is scarce."

At this moment an immense alligator, with a body apparently nearly as big around as a barrel, who had been standing on the bank intently watching the boat as it passed, waddled hastily into the water, and swam directly after it. Coot saw the approaching creature, and, with a sudden exclamation, he began to tug wildly at the oars. Phil seized the rifle, and turned toward the alligator.

"Don't fire!" screamed Coot. "You'll rile him awful! You'll rile 'em all! Put down the gun!"

Unwillingly Phil laid down the rifle, and Brewer rowed as hard as he could. The alligator did not pursue them long, but soon disappeared beneath the surface of the water; but this did not allay the fears of the oarsman.

"He ain't gin up yet," he gasped. "He'll come up in a minnit, right under us, and then over we'll go!"

"Don't fire!" screamed Coot.

This was not a cheerful prospect, and the boys would have assisted in the rowing had there been any spare oars.

But although Mr. Brewer was a small man, he was very vigorous, and he pulled away bravely. At the end of about five minutes of this violent exercise he stopped and rested.

The big alligator had not reappeared, and at the point where they then were there were no alligators to be seen either in the water or on the shore.

Coot looked around him. On the right hand of the stream the shore was low and marshy, but on the side nearest the town, the bank was a little higher than it had been, and between the creek and the forest, about a quarter of a mile away, there was a level stretch of dry land, covered with coarse grass.

"I tell you what we kin do," said Coot. "There's a road over thar in the woods that leads straight to town. 'Taint much of a road, but it'll do to walk in, and it won't be long before we kin strike it. I say, let's land here, and walk to town. We kin git thar easy in three or four hours."

"What do you mean?" cried Phil. "Leave this boat here, and the sail-boat in the river?"

"Yes, sir," said Coot. "You don't ketch me goin' down among all them 'gators ag'in. I wouldn't do it for all the money in the world! We kin come after the sail-boat to-morrow, and as for this dinky, we'll have to leave her. It's a pity for Bill Hawkins to lose his dinky, but what's a little boat like this to being scrunched up by a lot of 'gators!"

"It will be a mighty mean thing to leave the man's boat here!" exclaimed Phil, "and I'm not going to do it!"

"Nor I either!" cried Chap and Phœnix, in a breath.

"All right!" said Coot, pulling toward the shore. "I'm goin' to land and walk to town, and if you choose to run back through all them 'gators you kin do it. I ain't got no way to hender you."

"What did you come for, if you're afraid?" asked Chap.

"I didn't think there was so many of 'em, or I wouldn't 'a' come," was the cool reply.

When the boat touched the bank he put down the oars and jumped ashore.

"I'll take the shot-gun," he said, "'cause I don't want to lose any of John's things. And you might as well give me them victuals you've wrapped up, for if the 'gators don't eat you, you'll git to the boat before you're hungry; and I'm likely to want something on the way."

The gun and the luncheon were handed to him

without a word, and he began to make his way over the level ground toward the woods.

Chap and Phœnix now each took an oar, and pushed off, while Phil sat in the stern.

"Did you ever see such a good-for-nothing, contemptible coward as that, in all your life?" said Chap, not waiting until Coot should be entirely out of hearing.

"I never did," said Phil.

"Nor I," added Phœnix. "But for one, I'm glad we're rid of him. He wasn't a bit of good to us. And now, what are we going to do?"

"Go back to the boat as soon as we can, I should say," said Phil.

"Right through the alligators?" said Chap.

"There isn't any other way that I know of," replied Phil; "and we might as well do it first as last."

"All right," said Chap and Phœnix; and turning the boat, they began to row down stream.

"You'd better go slowly when you get among them," said Phil; "and of course we won't fire at them. I guess that Coot was right when he thought that it wouldn't do to rouse their angry passions when we are among them."

"It is a shame to leave all those splendid teeth and hides here, but I suppose it can't be helped," said Chap.

"I'd rather leave the teeth here than to have them in me," said Phœnix; "and I guess I

20

wouldn't want to wrestle with an alligator for his hide, either."

They soon reached the part of the creek where the alligators began to be numerous, and as they rowed on, they found that the sun had got higher, and as the day had become warmer the number of the ugly creatures who were basking in the sunshine was much greater than before.

The boys rowed very gently,.and the alligators paid but little heed to the boat, except as they regarded it as an object of curiosity.

Many of them seemed engaged in crossing the stream, and Phil frequently called out to the boys to slacken up a little or they would run into the lazy fellows.

On the banks some of them were lying perfectly still, as if they were asleep, while others moved sluggishly about, occasionally turning their heads and yawning, opening their great mouths so wide that the boys could see half-way down their throats.

Sometimes the boys were quite frightened, especially when the swimming beasts came near them; and once, when an enormous fellow rose close to the boat, and suddenly turning gave it a tremendous stroke with his tail, the boys thought, for an instant, that it was the creature's intention to upset them. But the blow was not repeated, and they breathed easier.

It was impossible, however, to look upon the horrid heads and writhing bodies of these great, lizard-like creatures without disgust and fear, especially when they were so numerous and so near.

"Nobody can say we haven't seen alligators," said Chap, as the boat slowly moved on.

"No, indeed!" said Phœnix; "but as far as I am concerned, I never want to lay eyes on one again."

"Look at that wretch!" exclaimed Phil. "I really believe he was going to take hold of your oar."

"I hope none of them will do that," said Chap, looking round apprehensively, "for I want to get out of this, and I don't want to trust to floating down, either."

Fearful as the boys were that they might at any moment run afoul of some bad-tempered creature, they kept steadily on, and at last, in safety, reached the mouth of the creek.

Even here an occasional alligator showed itself, but the boys took no notice of these, and rowed swiftly toward The Rolling Stone.

"Hurrah, boys!" cried Chap, when they had made the small boat fast to the other. "Now, at last, we are masters of our own vessel! This is splendid! Nobody on board to tell us what to do!"

"It won't be so splendid," said Phœnix, "if we can't get her up to town."

"But we can," cried Phil. "I can sail a boat better than that Coot Brewer."

"You'll have to do that," said Chap, "or I won't go along with you. I don't think Coot knew anything about sailing. How he is going to get his boat down to his brother's is more than I know. His business in life is to hunt alligators."

"Yes," said Phil, "and to do it the way he likes he's got to go where game is scarce."

"And that's in the woods," said Phœnix.

Phil had had a good many lessons in sailing a boat from his uncle, Mr. Godfrey Berkeley, and all the boys had profited greatly by observing Adam's method of managing the boat, consequently they felt quite delighted to have the opportunity of doing some sailing for themselves.

Phil went to the helm; Chap took charge of the main-sheet line, and Phœnix made himself generally useful at the main-sail and the jib.

The wind had got around to the east, and this was much in their favor. They pulled up the anchor, hauled up the sails, and set off bravely.

Phil was a careful fellow, and watched for every flaw of wind, and Chap was very prompt to let out the sheet as soon as ordered.

"I want you to understand, Phil," said Chap,

"that as I am captain, I give you orders to let me know every time you want the main-sheet let out."

"All right, captain," said Phil. "Discipline must be maintained."

"Boys," remarked Phœnix, "I wish we had shot some alligators. We might have done it after we got to the mouth of the creek."

"Perhaps that's so," said Phil; "but I was too anxious to get out from among them to think of anything else. I'd given up the shooting business."

"I'm afraid we were a little scared," said Chap, "and that we'll be laughed at when we get back without having fired a shot."

"Let them laugh," said Phœnix. "It won't hurt half as much as to have an alligator chewing at your legs."

20*

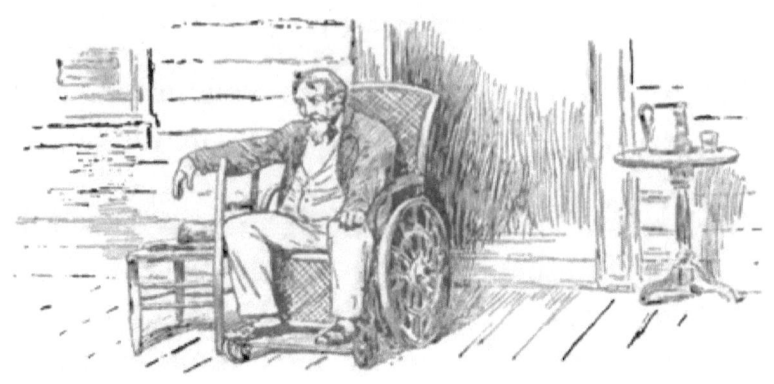

CHAPTER XXVI.

THE MAGGIE COMES TO TOWN.

Had Adam Guy been at the helm of The Rolling Stone, it would probably have reached the pier at Titusville a couple of hours sooner than it did under the guidance of the three boys. But it reached there finally, and our young friends were too glad to have made a safe passage to grumble about the slowness of it.

When the story about the alligators and the desertion of Coot was told at the hotel, it created a good deal of merriment and also some hearty condemnation of Brewer, who had not yet arrived in town.

Adam came up to the hotel, having seen the boat come in, and when he heard the story he was very indignant.

"I never oughter let you go with such a miserable good-for-nothin' feller. He thought of nothin'

but savin' his own wretched skin, and I've a great
mind to thrash it all off of him as soon as I ketch
sight of him."

"Don't do that," shouted the colonel, "for then
he can't get away, and we don't want him here.
This is the last time Coot Brewer ever takes anybody in a boat from this town."

Adam was just about to leave the house, being
anxious to finish that day the job of work he had
undertaken, when he stopped on the piazza, and
called out,—

"Hello! Here comes the dirty Maggie."

At this everybody came out. The story of the
boat-thieves had been told, and had excited a good
deal of interest. The young men had come from
parts unknown, and had been regarded with dis-
favor in the town before they started on their river
trip. They had hired a boat of a negro, no one
else being willing to trust them with one.

"They've been a long time getting here," said
Phil.

"I shouldn't wonder," said Adam, "if they'd
been a-hangin' back till we got away."

"That's so," said the colonel. "And now you
fellows make yourselves scarce, and keep out of
the way till they come up, and then we'll hear
what they have to say for themselves. If they
see you, I shouldn't wonder if they put off
again."

Our friends then retired into the dining-room, where, with doors shut and shutters partly closed, they watched the approach of the Maggie.

The dirty little boat sailed slowly toward the town, and when it reached The Rolling Stone, which was moored some little distance out in the river, it stopped, and the two young men seemed to be carefully examining her. Apparently satisfied that everything belonging to our friends had been taken out, and that they had probably gone on their way, they came up to the pier, and soon reached the hotel. The colonel was sitting on the piazza, not far from the dining-room window.

"Well," said he, as the two fellows, now more untidy than ever, ascended the steps, "you've got back, have you?"

"Yes," said one of them, "here we are."

"Did you shoot much?" asked the colonel, gazing at them steadfastly.

"Shoot!" cried the one who did the talking. "We didn't do none at all. Our guns was stole. The fellers that took 'em said they'd leave 'em with you, and I hope you've got 'em."

A number of persons had now collected on the piazza, and the three boys and Adam were listening intently in the dining-room.

"Your guns stolen!" shouted the colonel. "You must be a pretty couple of fellows to let your guns be taken from you."

"There was four of 'em that took 'em," said the other, "and they was too many for us."

"I should think half a good man would be too many for you two," said the colonel, who was beginning to talk louder and louder. "How did they come to steal them?"

"They just wanted 'em, and they took 'em," was the answer.

The other young man now considered it necessary to put in a word:

"We wasn't just about when they took 'em. If we had been, they wouldn't——"

"Shut up!" roared the colonel. "I can't stand any more such lying. I know all about you, and I know your guns were not stolen from you, and that you stole John Brewer's sail-boat, with everything in it."

"We didn't steal no boat," was the surly reply. "That was a lie them fellers made up."

"You didn't, eh?" cried the colonel. "I've some witnesses on hand that'll say something about that."

Then, turning to the dining-room window, he shouted, "Come out here!" and immediately Adam and the three boys appeared.

"Now, then," said the colonel, "will you say before these persons that you did not steal a boat from them?"

At first the two young men seemed utterly dismayed at the sight of the three boys and the man from whom they had stolen the boat, and whom they supposed were now far away. But as one of them fixed his eyes on Chap his dismay seemed to change into anger. His face grew very red, and he shook his fist at our long-legged young friend.

"There's the feller," he cried, "who tried to kill me! He fired a gun straight at me, and not a dozen feet away, and I a-doin' nothin'. It's all very well to talk about a little trick we played on 'em about the boat, but here's a feller who tried to murder me. If there's any law in this land I'll have it on him!"

The colonel turned to Chap.

"Is that so?" he said.

Chap admitted that the main facts were true, and then explained how it had all happened, but the colonel interrupted him, and leaning forward in his chair, as if he would jump out of it, he shouted at him,—

"I wouldn't have believed it of you! If there was a court sitting in this town, I'd have you brought before it this very day. I'm ashamed to have you in my house. If ever there was a boy who deserved being clapped into jail, it would be the one who fired at that fellow and didn't hit him! If I had my way I'd put you into prison till you learned to shoot."

At this there was a great roar of laughter from everybody except the two young men, and to these the colonel now addressed himself.

"There's been a good many scoundrels in these parts, since I've lived here, but I never see any to beat you two. You steal other people's property, and then you come here, and, right to my face, charge honest men with taking your things. I don't believe you ever owned anything in your lives. And you want your guns, do you? Well, you hired them of Jim Randall,—I know all about it,—and you'll pay for them from the day you took them till this minute."

One of the men attempted to say here that he hadn't had them for ever so long.

"Shut up!" roared the colonel. "You don't suppose I'm going to let Jim be cheated out of his money, do you, just because other people had to take care of the guns to keep you from doing mischief?—Bob!"

In a moment the negro boy appeared, and the colonel said to him,—

"Go tell Jim Randall to come right here.—As soon as you've paid him," he continued, turning to the young men, "you get out of this place. If the court sat this month, I'd have you up before it, but we're not going to keep you here at the public expense, and you've got to make yourselves scarce. And I want every man, woman, and child in this town to understand," he said, looking around at the people, "that not one of them is to harbor these fellows for a minute, or to speak to them, or to have anything to do with them. Here, Jim," he said, as that individual approached, "what do these scamps owe you for your guns up to to-day?"

Jim mentioned the sum.

"Pay it!" was the command of the colonel to the young men. "Now pay for your boat. Here's the man you hired it of. Now go!" roared the colonel, when this last order had been obeyed.

The young men had brought a couple of knap-sacks with them from the boat, and picking these up, they went. They had sense enough to see that there was nothing for them to do but to obey the autocrat of Titusville.

These two miscreants had not been gone more than half an hour before Coot Brewer wandered into the town. He was very tired, and looked warm.

When he entered the hotel, he was greeted with shouts of derision, and the colonel at once began to storm at him.

"Coot Brewer!" he cried, "if ever you take anybody in a boat again from this place, I'll have you horsewhipped!"

Coot sat down, and smiled a languid smile.

"You don't ketch me takin' out city chaps like them," he said. "They draws 'gators."

At this another shout of laughter arose.

"You dunderhead!" cried the colonel. "Don't you know that if you'd fired at them, every 'gator would have skedaddled?"

"Yes," said Coot, "a-carryin' off us fellers in their jaws."

Scolding and derision had very little effect on the brother of John Brewer. The colonel roared out his strongest condemnation of Coot's conduct in deserting the boys, and everybody laughed at him for being afraid of the alligators, but the placid Coot smiled through it all. He had got safely away from the 'gators in Lowper's Creek, and he did not care what happened now.

Just before supper, there was another arrival in the town. This was the yacht containing the family-party which the boys had seen on Indian River.

They came up to the hotel in a little procession, with their bundles, their valises, their baskets, their umbrellas, their fishing-rods, their canes they had cut, the little alligators they were carrying home in boxes, the shells they had picked up, and all the curious things they had gathered on their trip.

The colonel sat, with an austere countenance, and watched them approaching. They had not stopped in Titusville when they passed through before, having gone directly on board the boat, which they had engaged by letter, and it soon appeared that they did not intend to stop now.

The Winkyminky was to start early the next morning from Salt Lake, about seven miles away, and the head of the party considered it wise for them to go on that night to a house some three miles nearer the lake, so that they could the more easily reach the steamboat in the morning.

"All right," said the colonel. "Take the wagon and go along. I don't want anybody here that don't want to stop."

After supper, the colonel called Adam and the boys to him.

"Look here," he said. "You fellows have got to be sharp, or you won't get off in the Winky-minky to-morrow. She's a little tub, and don't hold many people, and there's a party down at the lake now, camping out, waiting for her. If this caravan, with their baskets, and bundles, and boxes of shells, get aboard first, there'll be no room for you, and you'll have to wait over a week. They hadn't any right to come back before they said they were going to. I know Captain Root like a book, and if you get there first with a note from me, he'll take you in, no matter who comes after you."

"We can't stay here another week!" cried the boys, in consternation.

"All right," said the colonel. "You be up early, and I'll put you through."

CHAPTER XXVII.

THE RACE THROUGH THE WOODS.

THE boys and Adam were awakened very early on Wednesday morning by Bob, and the colonel gave them scarcely time enough to eat their breakfast.

A wagon and two mules were at the back entrance to the hotel, and the colonel, bidding them a hasty good-by, told them to tumble in and be off.

"You've got to go lively," he cried, "to get ahead of those caravaners. And now, you Pete," he shouted to the negro driver, "you make them mules git!"

Pete whipped up, and away went our party along the sandy road that led out of Titusville. For a great part of the way the road lay through vast pine woods, where but few signs of life of any kind could be seen.

Before very long, they came in sight of the lonely house where the "caravaners" had stopped, and Pete whipped up his mules, hoping to pass the house before the party started; but this hope was vain; for, before they got to the gate, two carts, each drawn by one horse, came hurrying out, and immediately took the narrow road, on which there was but room enough for a single vehicle.

The two carts were piled high with people and baggage; but the horses were put to a gallop, and away they went, jogging and jolting over the rough road. Pete whipped up and galloped after them.

"If we'd started three minutes sooner," said Adam, "we'd been ahead of 'em, and been aboard long afore they got there. Them horses can't keep up that runnin'; but they can block the road for us, and that's just as bad. A lot o' people like that, just cruisin' round for pleasure, ain't got no right to swoop down without givin' any notice, and swamp other folks that's got no time to lose."

"Never mind," said Pete, who was keeping his mules close to the tail of the hindmost cart. "There's a place up here where I can pass 'em, and then you'll see me cut ahead."

In a few minutes an open place in the woods was reached, where, for a short distance, there were two wagon tracks side by side, the road having been changed, the original track being in a soft place, and full of ruts and mud-holes.

The moment he reached this old road, Pete dashed into it, whipping his mules into their wildest gallop. The wagon bumped and jolted over the rough places, the valises nearly bouncing out, while the boys were obliged to hold fast to their seats.

The horses and the carts were put to the top of their speed, and having the best road, seemed likely to keep ahead of the wagon. But Pete was not to be defeated. He had waited patiently for this opportunity of passing, and he was bound to pass. The tough muscles of his mules seemed able to pull the wagon at full speed over any road, without a thought of tiring, while the horses and the heavily-laden carts were beginning to flag.

With a crack of his heavy whip and a yell of triumph, Pete plunged ahead, and dashed into the other road a dozen yards in advance of the foremost cart.

"Hurrah!" cried Adam. "Now we can cut right along for the boat."

"Dat's so," said Pete, his eyes sparkling and his mouth in a broad grin. "We's done beat 'em! Dere ain't no other place where they can pass, even if they could kitch up."

21*

"Which they can't do," said Adam. "There ain't no more run in them horses."

The three boys looked back. In the front cart was an old gentleman and an elderly lady, apparently his wife. These sat on one seat, while another lady, holding a little girl, sat on some luggage, and the driver, a negro boy, perched himself on a trunk in the front of the cart.

In the second cart were two ladies, a short gentleman, in blue-flannel shirt and high boots, and a number of children, apparently all girls. These were piled upon valises and various articles of baggage, and altogether made a pretty heavy load for one horse.

The hindmost cart now stopped, and the gentleman and two or three of the girls got out and walked to ease the poor horse. Both carts then came on at a slow pace, the party evidently having given up the hope of reaching the steamboat in time to be well accommodated.

The boys now looked at each other.

"Look here!" said Phil.

"Fellows!" exclaimed Chap, at the same moment.

"That's so!" said Phœnix, as if he had known what the others were thinking of.

"Stop!" cried Phil to Pete.

The astonished negro drew up his mules, and Adam looked around.

"Let's take some of those children in here," said Phil.

"That's so," said Chap. "That's just what I was going to say."

"Plenty of room here," said Phœnix. "A big wagon, and no baggage to speak of."

"Yes," said Phil, "and I think it would be a mean thing for us to go ahead, and get good rooms on the boat, and cut out all these ladies and children."

"Mean!" said Chap. "It made me feel like a boat-thief when we passed them. Let's have them come along and get the best accommodations they can. We can stow ourselves away anywhere. Overcoats will do for beds, and our bags for pillows. It's only a three-days' trip. What do you say?"

"I say do it, of course," answered Phil.

"So do I!" said Phœnix, emphatically.

Adam listened to all this, and then, with a smile, he said,—

"All right, if you all say so; but you'll find pretty hard quarters if the boat is crowded and you've got no beds."

"Oh, we'll get along," said Chap. "Let's go tell them."

And the three boys jumped out of the wagon, while Pete was heard to make some remarks which seemed to indicate that, without knowing it, he had undertaken to drive a load of idiots to the Winkyminky.

The party in the carts seemed much surprised when the wagon stopped, but when the boys came back and made their offer to carry some of the children in the wagon, they were as much pleased as astonished, for they were feeling very much discouraged, having an idea that they were now going to have a pretty bad time on board the steamboat, and that she might even start off without them when the wagon reached her, and all her spare room was occupied.

"Much obliged to you," said the gentleman in the blue shirt, who was the father of the children. "It will help us ever so much if you will take a couple of these girls into your wagon. I'm afraid our horses will give out. We were talking about turning back, for I don't believe the Winkyminky has got more than two vacant state-rooms."

"Oh, I guess we can all crowd aboard!" said Phil, cheerfully. "At any rate, we'll try. We did think of going on ahead, but afterward made up our minds it would be better for all of us to go on together."

"It is very kind of you," said the gentleman, looking steadfastly at the boys. "It is necessary for us to travel on as fast as possible. This outdoor life does not suit my father," pointing to the old gentleman ahead, "as we hoped it would, and we want to get him to Jacksonville, where he can have more comfortable quarters."

"Why don't the old gentleman and the ladies get into the wagon?" said Chap. "We can pile into the carts, or walk. I think it is better to walk than to ride over these roads."

This proposition was demurred to, but the boys insisted, and although the old gentleman and his wife declined to leave their seats in the cart, it being difficult for them to get in and out of vehicles, the three ladies and the girls were induced to get into the wagon, which Adam cheerfully vacated to give them more room.

The procession now moved on, the gentleman with the blue shirt, who carried a gun, walking with Phil, while Adam and Phœnix walked close behind the wagon, to pick up any of the little girls who might fall out.

Chap strode ahead of all. He liked to walk alone, and look about, and make observations for himself, and besides this, he happened to remember that he was captain of the Rolling Stones, and that, whenever it was practicable, it was proper for him to be in advance.

When they reached Salt Lake they found the little steamer lying about a quarter of a mile from the shore, on which there was no sign of pier or landing-place.

The wagons and carts drove directly into the

lake, the bottom being hard sand, and splashed along to the Winkyminky. When they reached it, the water was a little over the hubs of the wheels, and when the vehicles in turn drove up to the side of the boat it was easy, even for the old gentleman and his wife, to step directly on to the lower deck. There was a small flat-boat near the shore, into which the pedestrians got, and a negro boy poled them to the steamboat.

The little Winkyminky was very much crowded, there being a dozen passengers on board when our friends arrived, but the old couple and the ladies were accommodated with beds, the captain giving up his room ; the children were to be stowed into various corners, while the men and boys cheerfully undertook to find places to sleep when night came.

At first the boys wondered that larger steamboats were not put upon this line, so that passengers could be more comfortably accommodated, but they had not gone very far before they found why the Winkyminky was so small.

CHAPTER XXVIII.

A PLOT AGAINST CHAP.

WHEN everybody who was going had leisurely gone on board the little steamboat, and the two or three negroes who were not going had deliberately got off into the flat-boat, and the engineer and fireman had followed the example of everybody else on board, and had gone to take a look at Adam's little bears, which he had brought with great care from Titusville, stowed away in the front part of the wagon, and when there really seemed to be no reason why a start should not be made, the anchor was hauled up and the engineer signalled to go ahead.

Among the passengers were the two young men who had stolen the boat; but they kept as much out of the way as possible, appearing especially anxious to avoid Adam and the boys. They spent most of the time in the engine-room and lived with the crew, probably hoping that by so doing the story of their misdemeanors and banishment from Titusville might not be told on board.

The boys, however, knew that they were on the boat; but, as they had not the slightest desire either to speak to them or look at them, the two miscreants were avoided quite as much as they wished to be.

After leaving the lake, which is a small body of water, the boat entered a narrow stream, which twisted and turned and bent back upon itself in such curious loops and curves, that few persons would have supposed it navigable by a steamer, until they had seen the Winkyminky perform the feat.

Sometimes the turn was so sudden that the bow of the boat almost touched the back, while the stern barely swept clear of it at the other end of the curve. In such cases the engine was stopped, and the boat pushed around the curve by the negro hands with long poles, which they thrust against the bank.

Often when they had just pushed the boat around one curve, they had to run to the other side of the deck to pole her around another, which bent in an opposite direction. None but a very small vessel would have made the necessary turns, and the boys were not surprised at her size when they saw the peculiar work she had to do.

Anything larger than that could not have got along that stream at all. Even after they at last got into the upper waters of the St. John's, the river was, at some points, very narrow.

The country they passed through was almost entirely uninhabited, although they sometimes stopped at a lonely wharf to take on vegetables or fruits, which were brought from the hummock farms, generally lying a little back from the river.

Alligators were plentiful along the banks. Water-fowl and other birds were in great numbers everywhere, and the boys had a very good time fishing for black bass from the stern of the little steamer. They caught enough to supply everybody on board with fresh fish during the entire trip, and many of the passengers, including the gentleman in the blue shirt, spent most of their time shooting at the alligators and birds.

The captain was a pleasant man, and talked a good deal with the boys.

"It seems pretty hard," he once said to them, "to get a boat along this narrow and crooked stream, but there are times in the year when I have no trouble at all. When the waters are high all this flat country is overflowed, and, as my boat only draws two feet of water, I sail right straight along over all this land that you see here, and pay no attention at all to the bed of the stream, wherever it may happen to be."

After a slow passage of two nights and parts of three days, they entered a broad lake, on one side of which was situated the town of Enterprise, and on the other that of Sanford.

Without stopping at the first, they proceeded to the last-named place, and the boys had scarcely scrambled upon the long pier when they were met by a portly gentleman, in a white necktie and broad straw hat, who, after asking their names, handed Phil a telegram. Phil hastily tore open the envelope, and read the following message:

"To Philip Berkeley, Sanford, Florida: Telegraph to Inman House, Jacksonville, by what boat you leave Sanford. Call there on arrival. JOHN ROBINSON."

This was a message sent by Mr. Godfrey Berkeley, and put in charge of a gentleman with whom Mr. Berkeley had an acquaintance, and who resided at Sanford. Mr. Berkeley knew that the boys must stop at this place in coming from the Indian River, and there had been time to write to the gentleman, as well as to telegraph. He and Helen did not wish the boys to know that they would meet them at Jacksonville, and the message was sent so as to make it sure that the boys would not be missed when they arrived at that place.

Phil and his two friends were very much surprised when they read the message, for they could not imagine who John Robinson might be. When they made inquiries in regard to this point of the stately gentleman, that individual waved his hand and raised his eyebrows.

"It is not to be supposed," he said, "that I should be cognizant of the personality of the gentleman who sent this message. All I have undertaken to do was to meet every boat which arrived from the locality from which you set forth, and when I should have the honor of meeting you to deliver you the message. If there is anything more I can do for you, I hope you will command my services."

"I suppose," said Phil, "that this John Robinson is somebody in Jacksonville to whom our money has been sent, and he has telegraphed here so that we can go to him and get it."

The stately gentleman was further interrogated, but he dismissed all remarks relating to John Robinson with a majestic wave of his hand, and proceeded to other topics. He was very kind, however; took them all, including Adam, to his house to supper, and gave them a great deal of information in regard to their trip to Jacksonville.

After going over to Enterprise for some freight, the Winkyminky intended to proceed to Jacksonville, but they had been told at Titusville that it would be better to take a larger and faster boat, if they could do so. The William Von Glode, the stately gentleman informed them, would, by a fortunate concatenation of circumstances, leave Sanford at about eight o'clock that evening, and he advised them to take passage in her.

Some hours would elapse before the Von Glode started, and there was time enough for the boys to walk about the place.

Before supper, Adam, who knew people here, and had heard where he could get a good job of work in repairing and refitting a boat,—for he was a boat-builder as well as a sailor,—had gone to see about this business, and was returning, when he noticed the two boat-thieves sitting under a tree by the side of the road.

He did not wish to speak to these fellows, nor did he care to pass them without a word. They had their faces turned away from him, and as there was a high board fence behind them, Adam went through a gate into the lot enclosed by this fence, so that he might altogether avoid these two fellows.

The board fence was not a very tight one, and as in passing the place where they sat he was but a short distance from them, he heard some words which made him stop.

"The long-legged fellow is always keeping to himself," were the words that he heard.

Now, as Chap was pre-eminently a long-legged fellow, this remark instantly recalled to Adam's mind the captain of The Rolling Stone, and this suggestion was made stronger by the fact that Adam had noticed that Chap was very fond of separating himself from the company, and doing something on his own account.

If these men were talking about Chap, it could bode no good to that young man, and Adam wanted to hear what should be said. So he stopped.

"If I can git a hold of him," was the next remark, "I'll pay him off square."

"Yes," said the other one, "and I'd like to pay off that no-account sea-rat. If it hadn't been for him we'd 'a' had our guns."

"That's so," said the other; "but it won't do to tackle the whole lot of 'em. If we can git hold of the feller that knocked us into the water and fired at me, we can give him his share and the sailor's too."

"I'm bound to bag some kind of game," said the other, "and he suits me better than any. What we've got to do is to keep a sharp eye on him and we're pretty sure to git a chance. The boat don't start till after dark."

Adam did not care to hear any more. It was plain enough that the two men intended to be revenged on Chap, and, as usually happens, they were the more determined on vengeance because they had deserved all they had suffered.

The point now was, what could he do to prevent this piece of rascality? for something must be done instantly, and the important thing was to warn Chap.

If the boys could be kept together until they went on board the steamboat, there would be no further trouble, for he was certain that the two rascals did not intend to take passage on the Von Glode.

Having settled these points in his mind, he set off for the house of the stately gentleman, which was on the main street of the town.

CHAPTER XXIX.

HOW ADAM WAS BAGGED.

When Adam reached the house, the family had just sat down to supper, and that meal had been prepared for him in another room. He did not think it necessary to disturb the little company.

He asked one of the servants to give him notice as soon as the supper should be over, and then he sat down to his own meal.

Before very long he heard the sound of chairs pushed back from the table, and then the colored woman informed him that "the folks had done finished."

Instantly Adam arose and hurried to the front of the house. There upon the porch he saw Phil and Phœnix, and calling them to him, he hurriedly asked where Chap was.

"Oh," said Phœnix, "it don't take him long to

eat. He got through before any of us, and asked to be excused. I suppose there is something in the town that he wants to investigate."

Adam almost turned pale when he heard this.

Quickly informing the boys of the plot against their companion, he told them that no time must be lost in finding Chap and keeping him with them.

No one had observed which way he had gone, but from his habits and his love of the water, it was probable that he had strolled either up or down the shore of the lake.

"You run along that way," said Adam, "and mind you keep together, for if them chaps get hold of one of you alone, they may make it bad for him. I'll go down-shore. I ain't afraid of 'em."

And with this, the party separated.

On their different ways through the town they met several persons, but nobody had seen Chap.

Adam soon found himself in the woods, where there were open spaces among the trees near the water, which allowed him to hurry along quite rapidly and to see to a considerable distance. He was certain he was on the right track, for in the sand near the water he saw the print of shoes, with a peculiar crack across the sole of one of them, which he had often noticed when Chap was stretched at full length on board The Rolling Stone.

"Now we'll give it to him."

Greatly encouraged by this, he followed the track, and just as he vaulted over the trunk of a fallen palmetto, he caught sight of Chap some distance head. He was crouched down, examining something at the water's edge.

Adam was just about to call to him, when he was suddenly enveloped in darkness. Something had fallen over his head, which blinded and almost choked him.

Then, through the coarse bag which had been thrown over him, he heard the words, spoken close to his ear,—

"Now we'll give it to him."

And almost at the same moment a tremendous blow from a club fell upon his back and shoulder.

The two boat-thieves had been following Chap, intending to throw the bag over his head, and then punish him to their hearts' content; but, perceiving the approach of Adam, they had hidden themselves behind the roots of a fallen tree, and when the sailor had jumped over the trunk and stood close to them, with his back toward them, they determined to give him the first taste of their revenge.

The instant that Adam felt the blow, he turned upon the fellow who held the bag over his head, and twisted him around in the direction from which the blow had come. But the man with the club skipped around and dealt the sailor another blow. Thereupon, Adam, feeling that he was at a great disadvantage in being blinded, and having an assailant free to whang him with a club, instantly clutched the man he held with a firmer grip, and tripped him up, both falling heavily to the ground.

Adam was a good wrestler, and could easily have thrown himself on his antagonist had he so chosen, but, instead of doing this, he rolled over so that the man he held in his strong arms was above him. In this way it was not easy to strike him without hitting the other fellow.

It is possible that the man who held the bag around Adam's neck thought that he had, by his own skill, put himself above the sailor. At any rate, he raised his head, and said to his companion,—

"I can hold him here, and you run down and whang that long-legs. He hasn't heard us, and you can slip up behind him. Be quick, now!"

The other fellow then left, and, being barefooted, he moved silently down toward Chap.

As soon as there had been time for him to get a little distance away, Adam, who had been lying on the ground, as if thoroughly exhausted by his brief struggle, suddenly revived, and, giving himself a vigorous twist, turned the other fellow under him, and grasping him by the throat, tore the bag off his own head with a jerk. Then Adam, giving a great shout, which echoed through the woods, proceeded to pound the miscreant under him as if he desired to punish him not only for the crimes he had done, but for those he intended to commit.

Chap, who was busily examining a curious little sulphur spring, which was bubbling up near the edge of the lake, lifting the wet sand as if some living creature was buried beneath and trying to get out, raised himself up when he heard Adam shout, and turned around just in time to see the boat-thief close upon him with his club in the air.

Chap was not as strong a boy as Phœnix, but he was long-limbed, and very excitable, and his fiery energy gave him much advantage for a brief struggle. Without the slightest hesitation he made a dash at the man with the club, and springing to one side as the blow fell, he threw his long arms around the fellow's waist. The club, of course, was of no use in such a close encounter, and dropping it, the man made a grasp with one hand at Chap's neck and throat. But Chap, as Phil had often said, was a fellow full of hinges, and jerking himself back to avoid this clutch, he did so with such suddenness that the man he held was pulled violently forward, while one of Chap's feet went down into the soft, bubbling sand he had been watching. Thus, losing his footing, Chap went over backward, and the man with him, and both were instantly rolling in the water and soft sand.

Chap was almost choked by the sand and water, but, throwing himself around like a wild cuttle-fish, he managed to get upon his knees and raise his head and body out of the water, which was not more than a foot deep, although he seemed to be sinking at least that far into the soft sand.

The man, who had loosened himself from Chap's grasp, was near him, and struggling to rise, his dripping face full of rage and astonishment. But Chap gave him no opportunity to do this. Throwing himself upon him he pushed the fellow backward till his head went down again under the water, but, not wishing to drown him, he jerked his head up again, and sitting astride of him began to harangue him.

The man was half lying down, with the water up to his chin, and vainly endeavoring to raise himself by his arms.

"So you were going to sneak up behind me and hit me with a club, were you, you cowardly scoundrel?" said Chap. "It would serve you right if I were to push you back and drown you."

"Let me up!" cried the man. "I'm sinking down into this sand. There's quicksands here, don't you know? Let me up! We'll both sink into 'em!"

"Let you up? Not I!" said Chap. "There's

a bubbling sulphur spring right under you, and I've a great mind to push you down into it. I believe you'd go slam-bang to the centre of the earth. I'm all right. I can feel solid ground on each side of you. I can just put my foot on you, and cram you down."

"Don't you do it! Don't you do it!" yelled the man, who was frightened almost out of his senses.

At this moment Adam appeared upon the scene. He had sufficiently punished his antagonist, and, having torn the bag into two strips, had tied him hand and foot with masterly sailor-knots. He had then hastened to Chap's assistance, but when he reached him he found that young man getting on very well without his aid.

He laughed when he saw the state of affairs, and then he stepped into the water, and helped Chap to his feet. The other fellow attempted to rise, but he was so embedded in the soft sand that he was unable to do so, and Chap and Adam reached into the water, and, each seizing him by one leg, pulled him out. Adam picked up the club the fellow had dropped in his struggle with Chap, and, seizing the man by the collar, made him rise to his feet.

"Now," said the sailor, "you come along with me, and if you give me any trouble I'll break your head."

The three then proceeded rapidly to the place

where the other rascal was lying, and, his feet being untied, Chap took him in charge, and the party set off at a good pace for the town, Adam relating to Chap by the way what he had heard and what had happened.

The stately gentleman was a magistrate, and before him the two fellows were taken, and when their attempted crime was told it created great excitement in the place. The men were committed to stand their trial at the next term of the court, which would be held in about a week.

Phil and Phœnix had returned while the examination was going on, and were as much astonished as Adam and Chap were to hear the magistrate say that the sailor and the young man who had been attacked must remain in the town to appear in the court as witnesses; otherwise, no charge could be proved.

"This is a bad piece of business," said Phil, as he stepped out on the porch.

"That's so," said Phœnix; "but none of us could have got off to-night, for the Von Glode has gone. She started before we got back to town."

"But we could have got off in a day or two," said Phil, "and now we may have to wait ten days or more. It is not likely this case will be the first one taken up. What do you think of it, Chap?"

But Chap was not there. He had vanished somewhere into the darkness.

CHAPTER XXX.

THE COUNTESS.

PHIL, Phœnix, and Adam were naturally much amazed by this second disappearance of Chap, which took place immediately after the magistrate's examination; but all conjectures and surmises were soon put to an end by the arrival of a note from Chap, which was brought by a negro boy. It was written on the back of a business card, and read thus:

"DEAR BOYS: I can't stay to any court. Let Adam testify. You can go away by the first boat that stops at Sanford. I am going to catch the Winkyminky. She starts from Enterprise to-night. I'll wait for you in Jacksonville. Good-by. CHAP."

The three gazed at each other in astonishment, as they read this note by a light in their host's hall, and when that gentleman came out to invite them to make their home in his house while they stayed in the town, they were obliged to tell him of their friend's disappearance. He was very much surprised at the information.

"He cannot take the Winkyminky," he said, "for that boat will not stop at this town to-night. Your young friend has been mistaken in his plans, and will probably return to the shelter of my roof ere long."

The boys knew Chap, and did not believe one word of this. They were greatly disturbed, and searched and inquired everywhere for news of him. They heard nothing, however, until about twelve o'clock, when a small boat, containing two negroes, came in from the lake, and the men reported that they had taken Chap out to meet the Winkyminky, and that when that boat had come along she had stopped and taken him on board.

"That's just like Chap," said Phil.

And Phœnix and Adam agreed that it was.

There was nothing for them to do but to wait till another boat should go down the river, and then to follow their captain, who, it must be admitted, had a rather curious way of leading his men.

As soon as Chap had heard what the magistrate said about his remaining as a witness, he felt that if he stayed in that room an instant longer he would be compelled, by some legal process, to appear at the next term of court, and he, therefore, slipped out of a side door and ran down to the river. The Von Glode was gone, but he felt he must get away from that town. Adam intended to stay there, anyway, and he could give all the testimony that would be needed; and as for Phil and Phœnix, they had seen nothing of the assault in the woods, and, therefore, would be free to leave by the first boat that came along. He was the only one that would be put to any trouble, and he must get away.

He remembered that the Winkyminky was going to Jacksonville, and he wondered if she had yet left Enterprise. If not, there might be some way of his getting across the lake, and taking passage in her. The money that had been advanced by the colonel had been divided, as Phœnix declined to be treasurer when he did not supply the funds, and Chap had enough with him to pay his passage.

At this moment a small boat, rowed by two negroes, came in from the lake, and Chap found that they had just come across from Enterprise.

The Winkyminky, they informed him, was preparing to start when they left, but she had not passed this point yet, and they could row him out to meet her. Chap then hastily wrote a note by the light of a lantern on the pier, and sending it to the boys, was taken out to meet the Winkyminky.

When that little steamboat came along the captain stopped and took Chap on board. His advent occasioned a great deal of surprise, but a comfortable state-room was given him, for all the Winky-minky's Indian River passengers had left her at Sanford.

But the next morning he found that there were three passengers who had come on board at Enterprise. One of these was an old gentleman, another was a very respectable negro woman; and the third was a lady.

The old gentleman was tall and thin, with a high shirt collar, and military bearing. He was a communicative person, and soon made friends with Chap, giving him a great deal of information on various subjects.

"Do you see that lady sitting over there by herself?" he said. "Well, sir, you don't often see anybody like that in this country, sir."

"What's the matter with her, sir?" asked Chap.

"Well, sir, she is a countess. Did you ever see one before?"

"Never, to know it," said Chap, "except in pictures."

"Well, that is one, sir. She is a republican by birth, from some place in the North, but she married a Spanish count, and they have an orange-grove in the back country here."

"Is it necessary for her to hold herself aloof?" asked Chap.

"Aloof!" said the old gentleman.

"Yes," said Chap; "she has been alone since I first saw her. I should think she'd be glad to have somebody to talk to."

"She might," said the other, "if she could meet with persons of her own rank and station. But, otherwise, she would probably prefer to be aloof, as you call it, sir."

About half an hour after this, Chap borrowed a fishing-line from the cook, for all his traps had been left at Sanford, and went to the stern of the boat, where the countess sat with a novel in her hand. Taking a position not far from her, he threw out his line, and let it troll behind the boat.

After awhile she raised her eyes from her book and, looking at Chap, asked,—

"What are you fishing for?"

"Good!" said Chap to himself. "She has broken through her feudal bonds, and speaks to the masses."

And then, aloud, he answered,—

"Anything I can get. Did your grace ever try trolling from a steamboat?"

"No," said the lady, with a laugh. "My grace never did. Why do you call me that?"

"It was the nearest I could come to it," said

Chap. "I should be glad to know just what to say."

"So long as we are not in Spain, madam will do very well," said the countess. "And now tell me, how did you come to get on board here, at night, all by yourself?"

Chap freely related the reasons for his coming on board the Winkyminky, which greatly interested the countess; and then, working backward with his story, he told what had happened since he left home. This account took a long time, and was only interrupted by the hauling in of one large cat-fish, which greatly horrified the countess, and induced her to ask Chap to put up his line and confine himself to his story, which she found more entertaining than her novel.

In spite of the fact that Chap did not belong to an aristocratic circle, the countess was very glad to talk to him, for he was the only person on board in whom she could take the slightest interest, and they soon became very well acquainted.

She was going, with her negro servant, to join her husband in Jacksonville, and had intended to take passage from Enterprise in the Von Glode; but she was too late for that boat, and was obliged to take the Winkyminky. This inconvenient little boat did not suit her taste at all; but she had to make the best of it, and was very glad to have on board such an original and pleasant boy as Chap.

CHAPTER XXXI.

A POINT OF HONOR.

NEARLY all that day the Winkyminky paddled bravely on her way, and then, all of a sudden, she stopped. A large cog-wheel, which was a part of her machinery, had broken. The engineer had known this wheel was going to break; but he hoped it would last till they got to Jacksonville.

Everybody was greatly disturbed at this accident, especially when the captain told them it could not have occurred in a worse place.

The Winkyminky drew but little water, and thus was sometimes enabled to make short cuts that a larger boat would not attempt, and, being a very slow craft, she saved distance whenever she could.

To avoid a long curve, she had gone inside of a wooded island, and here the accident had taken place. No large steamboat could come to her assistance here; but the captain said that the Rosa, the only small boat that would leave Jacksonville that week, would probably be along in a day or two, and would, most likely, pass inside the island. Then, he said, he would see what he could do to prevail upon her to turn back and tow his boat to the city.

This was poor comfort to the passengers, and they grumbled greatly; but nothing came of the grumbling, and they went to bed that night with the steamboat anchored near a small island, which shut it out from view of the body of the river, while the main shore, a hundred or more yards away, was wild and uninhabited.

In the morning it was found that they were out of fresh water, but the captain said that about half a mile down stream, on the main shore, there was a spring, and having put a barrel on board a small boat, he sent two of his hands to fill it with water.

Of course, Chap instantly demanded permission to go in the boat, and much to everybody's surprise, the countess also said that she would like to go. It would be a relief from the monotony of sitting in the anchored steamboat.

The promise of a small compensation made the two men very willing to row an extra load, and the countess and Chap, in company with the water-barrel, were pulled to the mainland. Here the two men set to work to fill the barrel, carrying the water in pails from the spring to the boat, and taking a good deal of time to do it, while Chap and the countess walked along the shore to survey the scene, the lady keeping a sharp lookout for any alligators that might be basking beneath the trees.

The countess was very much disturbed at the interruption to her journey.

"It is too bad," she said, "that we are obliged to stay in this horrid place, and on that wretched little boat. There is no knowing how long we will have to wait here. The next thing will be that we will have to send ashore for something to eat as well as water to drink, and what they'll find I'm sure I don't know."

"I should think they'd send to the city for relief," said Chap.

"I suppose they will eventually," the lady replied, "but they'll have to wait for a steamboat to come along to do that. I don't suppose they could row there."

At this moment she made an exclamation. They were now below the end of the island, and could see far down the river, which was here very wide. Two or three miles away was a large steamboat coming from the city.

"Oh!" cried the countess; "do you see that?

If I could only stop her, and get on board, I would go as far as she is going, and then come back in her to the city. Anything would be better than staying on that cramped-up little Winky-minky, with nothing to eat. I believe that would be the quickest way of getting to Jacksonville, and we would stop somewhere where I could telegraph to my husband. Oh! can't we signal her?"

"I'll row out to her!" cried Chap. "I'll stop her!"

And turning, he ran as fast as he could to the place where the boat was hauled up.

The men had just come down with a couple of pails of water, but when Chap promised them a dollar apiece to row him out to the approaching steamboat, they lifted out the barrel, half-filled with water, and attempted to push off the boat, but they found it stuck in the mud so tightly that it was almost impossible, and Chap raved and stamped at the fruitless result of their ill-managed efforts.

The countess was now walking rapidly toward them, but Chap, hoping in his heart that nothing in the rules of aristocratic circles would prevent a fellow from wading in the mud in a good cause, pulled off his shoes and stockings, rolled up his trousers, and plunged in.

By the united strength of the three the boat was soon afloat, and all jumped in. The negroes seized the oars, and Chap shouted to the lady that they would be back in no time.

"Don't fail to stop her!" cried the countess. "Tell them I'll pay them for all the time they lose. It is the Humphrey Giles. The captain knows me."

The boat left the shore so rapidly that Chap scarcely caught the last of these words. He suddenly remembered that he was leaving a lady alone on the shore.

"I never thought," he said, "that she would be there all by herself."

"Dar's nuffin' dar to hurt her," said one of the negroes, who was afraid Chap might change his mind and turn back, and so make them lose their money; "and we ain't got no time to take her on if ye want to ketch that boat."

"That's so," said Chap; "and now give way, my hearties!"

Chap had read tales of man-of-war life and of whaling voyages, and he knew that the way to make men row hard and fast was to yell and shout at them like mad, and for work of this kind no one was better adapted than the captain of the Rolling Stones.

The negroes became so excited that they made the boat spin over the water. It stopped directly in the course of the Humphrey Giles, when that boat was a quarter of a mile away.

24

Chap stood up in the stern, and frantically waved his hat, and shouted,—

"Stop!"

Perceiving that something was the matter, the captain of the great steamboat gave orders to slow up and back water, and as soon as she was stopped Chap was pulled to her side, and gave the news of the Winkyminky's disaster, and the message of the countess.

The countess was well known along the river, and apart from his willingness to assist the passengers of a disabled boat, the captain knew that he would be paid for any loss he might sustain by stopping.

He asked Chap where the Winkyminky lay, and then told him that he would go up to the other end of the island, and if the countess and other passengers who might want to go on board the Giles could be brought to him without delay, he would wait for them, but that not a moment of time must be lost.

At this instant a cry was heard from the upper deck.

When Chap heard that cry, he sprang to his feet, and nearly fell backward out of the boat. Well he knew the voice, especially when it called his own name.

"Helen!" he exclaimed.

And sure enough, there was Helen leaning over

the railing of the upper deck, and by her side was
Mr. Godfrey Berkeley.

When Chap saw his sister, he was at first utterly
astounded. He simply stood and looked at her.
Then he made a step forward to climb on board
the steamboat. Then, at the same instant, he
remembered the countess left on the lonely shore.
A brief but sharp struggle took place within
him.

The captain again called out that no time must
be lost, and that he could not wait long, and one
of the hands ordered his negroes to back away
from the steamboat.

As far as he was concerned, there was no reason
why he should not jump on board and rush to his
sister, who was saying all sorts of things to him
from above. But there was that countess! Oh,
how he wished that he had brought her along
with him! It would not do to trust those negroes
to go back after her. They would bungle everything, and never get to the Giles in time. He had
come on the lady's errand, and was bound in honor
to go back to her.

The bell in the engine-room tinkled, and the
negroes backed out of the way of the moving
wheels.

"I'll come back directly, Helen!" screamed
Chap. "I've got to fetch a countess! And
now you fellows lay yourselves out! Another

dollar apiece if you get us on board the Giles in time."

Chap exhorted and urged, occasionally turning to wave his hat to Helen, who shook her handkerchief at him until the island shut them out of sight of each other.

When Mr. Berkeley had received, in Jacksonville, a telegram directed to John Robinson, stating that the boys would leave Sanford in the William Von Glode, he and Helen had kept a sharp lookout for that boat, and when she arrived they were at her pier, and were greatly troubled at finding no boys on board.

Phil and Phœnix had never thought of telegraphing to Mr. Robinson that they had missed the Von Glode, and Mr. Berkeley could not imagine why they had not come. '

The gentleman with the blue shirt and the large family, who had come from Titusville, was on board, and he told Mr. Berkeley that the boys had certainly intended to come down on this boat, but just before she started he had heard something of a disturbance in the town, and as some disreputable characters were there, between whom and the boys there was an ill-feeling, he was afraid the young fellows had got into trouble, which had detained them.

Mr. Berkeley immediately telegraphed to his friend in Sanford, but as that gentleman happened to be out of town that afternoon, his wife put the telegram away, as she was accustomed to do with his letters, until he should return.

Receiving no answer, Mr. Berkeley and Helen took passage early the next morning on board the Humphrey Giles for Sanford. When they saw Chap in the stern of the little boat which had stopped the Giles, their astonishment was as great as they imagined it could be, but when he rowed frantically away to fetch a countess, their amazement was actually increased.

24*

CHAPTER XXXII.

CHAP IS DOWN UPON ARISTOCRACY.

WHEN Chap reached the spot where he left the water-barrel and the countess, he found the former sticking up in the mud, but there were no signs of the latter. Chap sprang into the mud, and struggled to shore. Where was she? He hoped she was waiting somewhere in the shade, but he could not find her. He called and shouted for her, but there was no reply. He was just giving himself up to despair, when one of the negroes cried out, "Dar she!" and pointed in the direction of the Winkyminky.

And there, sure enough, was the countess and her colored servant in a boat, just pushing off from the Winkyminky, while the whistle of the Humphrey Giles could be heard from the other side of the island.

The countess was a woman of action. As soon

as Chap had left her, she had run along the shore,
until she was opposite the Winkyminky, and
shouted for some one to come over for her. If the
Giles should consent to stop for her, she wanted to
take her maid and some of her baggage with her,
and there was no time to be lost. There was another boat on the Winkyminky, and it had been
sent for her, and it was now about to take her and
her maid around the upper end of the island to the
Giles, whose whistle gave sufficient signal that she
was there, and waiting.

"Upon my word!" ejaculated Chap, as he gazed
upon this scene. "Aristocrats and countesses,
indeed! Give me a republican form of govern-
ment!"

And he dashed through the mud, and into the
boat.

"Never mind the water-barrel," he cried.
"Row after that boat. Another dollar if you
catch it."

The negroes' arms already ached from the violent rowing they had done, and Chap's throat was
sore from his continuous shouting; but the men
bent again to their oars, and Chap's former yells
were nothing to what he uttered now. He felt
sure that if the countess's boat reached the Giles
before he did, that steamboat would start off without him, and his sister, whose appearance on board
was such an astounding mystery, would be carried

away from him. The captain would not wait for anybody after the countess was on board. His soul was fired with rage at that treacherous woman, for whom he had taken so much trouble to return, and for whom he had probably lost his chance of joining his dear sister. If he could catch up with her, he would tell her a thing or two.

"Tug at her! tug at her!" he shouted to the oarsmen. "Crack your backs! Break your bones! Give way, boys, give way! Why *don't* you pull? Jerk her out, boys! jerk her out!"

And the two negroes, with bare heads, perspiration rolling down their cheeks, and their eyes and teeth glistening, as they rose in their seats with every wild pull at the oars, did almost jerk the boat out of the water in their frantic efforts to earn the money Chap had promised them.

There was no rudder to the boat; but Chap sat in the stern, and by gestures and commands directed the oarsmen. He did not row toward the Winkyminky, but kept directly after the boat containing the countess.

There was nearly half a mile distance between them when they started, and the upper point of the island was certainly less than a quarter of a mile above the foremost boat. So Chap had great odds against him as far as regards distance, and there seemed much reason to fear that the countess's boat would round the point and reach the Humphrey Giles before Chap could be seen or heard; but the odds in other respects were somewhat in Chap's favor.

His men were now so thoroughly warmed up to their work that they forgot their arms had ached a little while before, and they pulled like tireless machines.

The other boat had two strong oarsmen; but it carried two passengers and some baggage, and there was no wildly excited fellow in the stern to urge, with ringing battle-cry, his men to deeds of valor.

Chap's boat steadily gained upon the other, and the few people who were left on board the Winkyminky cheered and clapped him as he passed. They did not know whether he wanted to go on board the other steamboat or not; but they saw plainly enough that he had some reason for catching up with the countess.

"I wish I knew how to make those fellows work like that," said the captain of the Winkyminky, as he watched Chap's boat. "They never pulled with such good will for me."

"Perhaps you could do it," said the old gentleman who was standing by him, "if you would make yourself a raving lunatic like that boy. I believe he has scared those black fellows out of their wits, and that they are trying to get away from him."

The countess did not perceive the boat that was following them, and she knew nothing about the Giles, except that it was on the other side of the island, where it was certainly stopping, and occasionally blowing its whistle.

The trees and high reeds prevented the countess's boat from being seen from the Giles, and, as the captain might not know that a boat was coming to him, he might start off at any moment. Therefore, the countess was anxious to get in sight of the Giles as soon as possible, and urged her men to row as fast as they could, her words, however, having nothing like the same effect as the yells of Chap.

When she went to the Winkyminky and then started for the Giles, she had no idea that she was behaving in a manner which Chap would consider treacherous. She did not know that he thought of going on board the Giles, and indeed he had said to her, when they were talking together, that he supposed he would have to stay by the Winkyminky until she was towed to the city. Of course the lady could not be supposed to imagine that the whole current of the boy's feelings and intentions had been changed by his finding his only sister on board the Giles.

There was a point of reeds which grew out into the water for ten or a dozen yards from the end of the island, and around these the countess's men rowed their boat as rapidly as they could.

The moment they were on the other side of them, and within sight of the waiting Giles, the countess waved her handkerchief above her head to attract attention to her approach.

The people on the steamboat had, of course, been expecting a boat to come to them, and they were looking for it to come around the end of the island. And we may be quite certain that no one watched for it with greater eagerness than Helen and Mr. Berkeley. Their grief and dismay, therefore, when they saw two women in the stern of the boat and no Chap, need not be described. Was he not coming?

If they could have looked through the reeds and bushes to the other side of the island they would have known that Chap was coming!

The moment that the foremost boat turned the point of reeds, Chap's frenzy doubled.

"Wake up!" he screamed. "Are you going to sleep, and have me left? Ten more pulls, and we've got her! Give way now! Give way! Tear at it, I tell you! Tear at it!"

They had now reached the reeds, but Chap had no intention of going around them. They were growing in the water, and the water would certainly float his boat.

"Pull around, you Bill," he cried. "Smash

right through them! Drive her through, boys! Drive her through!"

The tall reeds bent beneath the sudden dash of the boat and the wild sweep of the oars; and in a few seconds Chap's little craft was out in the open water beyond.

Just ahead of her, and not twenty feet away, was the countess's boat. Chap's men were rowing as madly as ever, and in a few strokes they would be upon it.

"Stop!" yelled Chap. "Back water!"

But these words had no effect on his two negroes. He had been shouting and yelling to them ever since they started, and they did not now notice what he said. They were so filled with savage excitement that they paid no attention to mere words.

The men in the other boat tried to pull out of the way, but they were not quick enough. Chap's boat crashed into that of the countess, smashing in one side, and nearly turning it over with the violence of the shock.

CHAPTER XXXIII.

WHICH FINISHES THE STORY.

WHEN Chap's boat dashed into that of the countess, it struck the latter craft on one side, near the stern, crashing into her as if she had been an earthen pot. The water would have instantly rushed in had not this broken side been lifted in the air by the violence of the shock, turning the countess and her woman into the water as neatly as if they had been slipped out of a ladle.

One of the oarsmen also went overboard, but the other one sprang to his feet at the moment of collision, and jumped on Chap's boat.

The two negroes who had been rowing Chap looked around, utterly dazed by the shock, while our hero, as pale as a sheet, sat speechless in the stern. He could scarcely believe that this dreadful thing had happened; but in an instant his face flushed, and he was on his feet.

About a yard from him, the face and arms of the countess appeared above the water. Chap's first impulse was to jump in after her; but, instead of doing that, he threw himself down flat in the boat, and stretching himself out from its side like an opening telescope, he seized the lady just as she was going down again. He was leaning so far out of the boat, that not only did he have no power to hold her up, but his head and shoulders went down also, their weight assisting her to sink. He would have gone entirely out of the boat if he had not hooked his toes into the boards at the bottom.

It is probable, however, that both he and the countess would have been drowned, for a boy might as well have his whole body under water as to have his head there, had not the man who had jumped from the other boat perceived the danger, and, slipping by the astonished oarsmen, who were looking behind them in the vain attempt to make out what had happened, seized Chap by the legs, and drew him in, bringing also the countess to the surface. The other men now sprang to the rescue, and the lady was lifted into the boat.

The moment she found herself in the air, she gave a great gasp and sank upon a seat, breathing hard and fast.

" All right?" anxiously cried Chap, his face and hair dripping with water.

The lady nodded and went on with her panting. She had been taught by her husband that if she ever fell into the water, the important thing to do was to hold her breath, and this she had done during the very short time she had been beneath the surface. But if she had not entirely forgotten to do anything else, she might have had a more comfortable time. The spot where she fell in was not over four feet deep, and if she had stood upon the bottom, her head would have been above the water; but her whole soul was possessed with the one idea of holding her breath, and she never thought of such a thing as trying to stand on her feet.

The negro woman and the man who had fallen overboard had speedily found a foothold, and had stood up, and, with dripping heads and faces, were now wading toward Chap's boat.

Into this they were helped, for the other boat had filled with water, and sunk.

The two valises of the countess were fished up from the bottom by one of the men, and deposited in the boat. The floating oars of the sunken boat were picked up, and the negroes proceeded to row Chap's heavily-laden craft toward the Giles.

All the condemnation of aristocratic institutions which Chap intended hurling at the head of the countess was entirely forgotten. He felt that her misfortunes had sufficiently established the fact

that even the highest rank and the proudest
lineage must sometimes give way before the rapid
advance of republican vengeance.

As for the countess, she said never a word.
She was entirely occupied in getting back her
breath, and in trying, with the help of her woman,
to put her hat and hair into decent order.

On board of the Humphrey Giles, there had
been a great deal of excitement and anxiety.

When the boat containing the shouting Chap
and his frantic oarsmen rushed out of the reeds,
and sprang like a wild beast on the other boat, the
people on board the Giles, who witnessed the
occurrence, gave a cry of horror.

The captain ordered a boat to be lowered to go
to the rescue, but before it could be got ready, all
the capsized people were in Chap's boat, and it was
being rowed toward the steamboat.

Helen, with great delight, recognized her
brother, but Mr. Berkeley was much troubled.
Where was his boy—his Phil? and where was
young Poole?

The Humphrey Giles was detained much longer
than her captain expected she would be. Everybody on board wanted to know all about what had
happened, but no one except Chap seemed able to
tell anything, and he was so busily engaged hug-
ging and kissing a girl in a straw hat, that he paid
no attention to the questions of anybody.

Mr. Berkeley, however, presently succeeded in getting the information that the two other boys were safe at Sanford. Then Chap's two oarsmen had to be paid, which took every cent he had, and then one of the men who had rowed the countess said his captain would want to be paid for the boat that was smashed.

This matter was soon settled by Mr. Berkeley agreeing to make compensation when they should get back to Jacksonville, and then, after a message had been delivered from the captain of the Winky-minky to the captain of the Humphrey Giles, requesting the latter to telegraph to the city the condition of the disabled steamboat, the Winkyminky's men rowed away in their boat, and the Giles proceeded on her way.

Chap's story was a long one, and had many eager listeners, but he did not begin it until he had fully satisfied himself how Helen and Mr. Berkeley happened to be there.

"I feel like another man," said Mr. Berkeley, when all had been told, "now that I know where Phil and Phœnix are."

"It would be just our luck," said Chap, "if those fellows should take some other boat and pass us, and go on to Jacksonville."

"You need not try to frighten me that way," said Mr. Berkeley. "No boat has passed us yet, and I have made arrangements with our captain to stop and hail any boat we may meet, night or day, until we reach Sanford. So I don't think we shall miss them that way."

"My gracious, Chap!" exclaimed Helen, when she had sufficiently recovered from her excitement to notice something more than the face of her dear brother; "do you wear knickerbockers? And what kind of stockings have you got on?"

"Why," said Chap, looking down below his rolled-up trousers, "those are not stockings. That is St. John's River mud. You see I've been wading, and, as for my shoes and stockings, I left them over on the bank, where I have been getting water. I don't cut a very handsome figure, do I?"

Mr. Berkeley and Helen gazed at the long-legged boy, who had lost his hat, and whose wet hair was sticking out in all directions, and they burst into a laugh, in which Chap unhesitatingly joined.

"I expect the people must have wondered," said Helen, "when they saw me kiss such an awful-looking boy, but I was glad enough to get the chance."

"We could all see that," said Mr. Berkeley; "and now I'll take him down below, and see what can be done for him."

When Chap returned on deck, washed, combed, and dressed in a complete suit, which had been

loaned him by the purser, he was a well-dressed
and very gentlemanly-looking person. He did
not see the countess that day, as she did not come
out from her state-room, but both he and Mr.
Berkeley made inquiries about her, and ascer-
tained that she had sustained no injury. But early
the next morning, just before the boat reached
Sanford, Chap saw the countess on the deck. He
went up to her, but she looked at him coldly, and
made no sign of recognition; but when he spoke
she opened her eyes.

"Are you the boy," she exclaimed, "who
stopped this steamboat for me?"

"And who afterward upset you in the river,"
said Chap. "Yes; all of me that isn't purser of
this boat is that boy."

"But how did you come to run into us that
way?" she asked.

Chap then explained how he thought he had
been deserted by her, and how, in his anxiety to
overtake her, the accident had occurred.

"Well," said she, when she had asserted that
she had no idea of treating him in that dreadful
way, "you gave me a bad wetting and a great
fright, but you also helped and amused me very
much, and, on the whole, I am glad I met you."

And she cordially shook hands with him.

"And now," said Chap, as he rejoined Helen,
"I'm done with the aristocracy. It will do very

well in certain quarters, but republican institutions for me."

Phil and Phœnix were on the pier when the Humphrey Giles arrived at Sanford. They had received a telegram from John Robinson the day before, sent from a point below on the river, telling them to wait at Sanford for the Giles. They had wondered at the message, and would have waited anyway, as there had been no chance for them to leave. But when Chap, handsomely dressed, appeared on the gang-plank, conducting Helen and Mr. Berkeley, Phil and Phœnix could not have been more astonished had they seen an alligator stand up on its tail and sing "The Last Rose of Summer."

"What grates on me," said Phil, laughing, as they sat on the porch of Mr. Berkeley's friend, the magistrate, "is to see Chap dressed up in that fine fashion, while Phœnix and I are going about in these old flannel clothes."

"You forget," said Chap, sitting up as straight as possible in his chair; "that I am your captain, and, therefore, ought to be better dressed. There is nothing that makes fellows knuckle down to rank and dignity like appropriate costume."

"Well," said Phœnix, "as we haven't knuckled down much so far, I suppose we might as well do it until the purser makes you take off his clothes."

"And when we get to Jacksonville," said Mr. Berkeley; "I will have you all refitted."

That afternoon, when the Humphrey Giles started northward, or down the St. John's River to Jacksonville, our friends were on board of her.

After some persuasion from Mr. Berkeley the worthy magistrate consented to let Chap go, and depend upon the testimony of Adam for the conviction of the two young men who had committed the assault.

That individual had sold his little bears to a man who was going North, and, having a good job of work, he did not wish to leave Sanford. He came down to the pier to see his former companions depart, and bade them a hearty good-by.

"It is a great pity, boys," said Helen, when they were all in the hotel at Jacksonville, getting ready to start homeward,—"it is a great pity that you brought nothing with you from your Indian River trip, not a shell, nor a sea-bean, nor even any of that beautiful Spanish moss which hangs from the trees."

"Helen," cried Chap, "what are you talking about? Don't you know that rolling stones gather no moss?"

And, majestically waving his hand, he walked away.

The homeward trip, though marked by no exciting incidents, was a delightful one for all the party; and the mail from Boontown, which carried to the colonel in Titusville a cheque for the amount due him by the Rolling Stones, also carried a full account of this journey in a letter from Helen to Mary Brown, the girl who could not remember ever having seen another girl.

THE END.